# NOW
# THAT'S
# WHAT
# I CALL
# CHAOS
# MAGICK

# NOW THAT'S WHAT I CALL CHAOS MAGICK

Greg Humphries

&

Julian Vayne

Also available
Seeds of Magick
Personal Development with the Tarot
The Inner Space Workbook
(all above titles Julian Vayne with Catherine Summers)

Pharmakon – Drugs and Imagination
(Julian Vayne)

For information about new publications and workshops please consult our on-line esoteric journal at

**www.liminalspace.co.uk**

Published by
Mandrake of Oxford
PO Box 250
OXFORD
OX1 1AP (UK)

A CIP catalogue record for this book is available from the British Library and the US Library of Congress.

**1869928741**

# NOW THAT'S WHAT I CALL CHAOS MAGICK

## Volume 1 & 2

First printed edition published by Liminalspace Publications.

Cover illustration: "Mercury Descending" by Greg Humphries

www.liminalspace.co.uk

Also available

Seeds of Magick
Personal Development with the Tarot
The Inner Space Workbook
(all above titles Julian Vayne with Catherine Summers)

Pharmakon – Drugs and Imagination
(Julian Vayne)

For information about new publications and workshops please consult **our on-line esoteric journal at**

**www.liminalspace.co.uk**

# Dedication & Acknowledgements

For Ronald - without whom this book would never have happened.

## Volume 1

This book is dedicated to all those wonderful people who shared the journeys documented in this text. The participants in the Fotamecus Film Majik Project, the twice born of the Kali puja sequence, The Anderida Grove of the Order of Bards, Ovates and Druids, all the players in PACT, The Illuminates of Thanateros, my lovely friends and my beloved partner. And for Osric.

I am indebted to a variety of sources both for ritual material and inspiration. I would particularly like to thank Fenwick Rysen, Brother rhino (who in turn draws on the work of various members of AMOOKOS) and Keyman whose work appears in this Volume.

## Volume 2

I have met so many wonderful people during the time it took to write this book, usually they were where I didn't expect to find them. Specifically I want to mention The Illuminates of Thanateros who have in their midst some of the most adventurous, creative and outrageously funny individuals I have ever had the pleasure, and pain, to work with.

Big Love to Rachel, Vanya and Eleanor, the unborn one, for whom this work was undertaken in the first place.

Ideas never wholly originate in one person so I hope I have credited the appropriate authors and work where I can. I have been particularly brutal with the ideas of Mantak Chia and John Seymour, and I hope they can forgive me for that.

# Contents

Greg Humphries & Julian Vayne

# Foreword

**by Dave Lee**

Our spells are forever the same, clothed in beliefs that change in accord with the times. Maybe there is, forever, Nothing on the other side of Progress, endless novelty spewed forth by the fertile void, the Ginnungagap,

Chaos. Those of us writing at this growing edge find ourselves mythologizing our personal dialogues with the Mystery, in the form of our feelings about the specifics of our lives.

To this book of illuminated stories that you hold, I would like to add my own, as a fulcrum for my own issue with the book. This tale stems from as late as last year; I heard of a speaker at an occult conference voicing distaste for Chaos Magic as if it was mere punkery past its time. I hadn't realised there were people around who still hadn't got the point - which leads me to the 'Chaos Magic is dead' theme in the present book. It's all very well to say CM is dead - I've used that as a strap line myself - but the fact remains that there are still those out there, who consider themselves magicians, who still prefer think it's some kind of infantile disorder cult. For anyone trying to do sorcery and yet suffering from this sad delusion, I would point out that if you want your magic(k) to succeed then you are probably already modelling other successful magicians of the past, and that this modelling approach is the core of the Chaos critique of magical method. Take note! Surely you wouldn't want people to think you're the kind of person who talks about Magick but does no work!

Another criticism levelled at Chaos Magic is that it presents magic as an unfettered discipline of Power, without an explicit scheme of self-illumination. This image was in itself generated by early exponents of Chaos Magic, so that perception is fine by me - and anyway, if you're writing a serious book on magic you're not seeking to be liked - just respected! And this book is very much the exception: The authors' mythologizing of their experience lends a vivid sense of personal evolution, an encompassing of their intimate lives in a total web of magical practice which takes in aspiration, illumination, purpose; the building of life and the preparation for an eventual good death.

Some of the material in this book led to my adding a couple of important strands to my own work. I'm delighted and grateful that anything published with the word magic(k) in the title these days can accomplish that.

# Volume 1

## What Is Chaos Magick?

In order to answer this question let's take a brief tour through the development of magick in the West...

The occult tradition has always been highly syncretic, embracing ideas, language, techniques and images from many different areas of human experience. In demonstrating such eclecticism and mutability one might well argue that, since the end of the shamanic phase of culture (in the West), occultism has clung like a rather disreputable parasite to the pelt of first religion and then science. The magicians of the medieval period couched their work in terms of Hebraic and Christian Qabalism. Alchemy and the Hermetic tradition maintained an uneasy truce (mostly) with Catholicism and latterly spiritualism attempted to clothe itself with a broadly Protestant iconography.

Today occultism is beginning to emerge on its own terms. For occultism is a study, an area of enquiry that, whilst it may utilise the language of religion or science (or art, or many other things), it is itself a complete body of knowledge. For me, as I have explained in my previous work *Pharmakon,* occultism *is the study and practice of engaging with mystery.* Magick is the technology of exploring the occult, those hidden aspects of the universe. Moreover magick provides mechanisms whereby we can learn to cause change in the hidden processes of the universe.

The grandfather of contemporary occultism is undoubtedly Eliphas Levi who attempted to formulate a general theory of magick (indeed he always claimed to be primarily a theorist rather than a practitioner of the occult arts). It was Levi's' *The Dogma and Ritual of High Magic* (1856) that began the process of de-coupling magick from a specifically religious viewpoint Levi sought, if not to create a scientific vocabulary for magick, then at least to try to cut through the complexity of the subject in order to identify 'principles'. Levi focused his work within what we might now call the Western magickal tradition, but contemporary researchers were also active in creating a scientific language (devoid of explicitly religious content) to explain such phenomena as mesmerism.

Levi's first magickal principle was that of the Will which, as in mesmerism, was imagined 'as steam or the galvanic current', that is a 'real' force. Levi opined that paraphernalia such as robes, incense, magick circles and the like were primarily important as aids in supporting the Will. Their virtue was in their effect on the Will of the magician and not primarily to be considered as arising from any inherent property. With this principle Levi, at a stroke, jettisoned the magicians reliance on virgin parchment and the blood of pigeons and recast the material mechanics of magick into what Israel Regardie would later call 'an artificial system of props and aids'.

Levi's second principle was that of the astral light. This light was the medium or dimension of reality which permeated all things, and of which the material world was only one of innumerable projections. Levi's conception of the astral light was similar to ideas such as that of the luminiferous ether (the medium through which electromagnetic radiation was conjectured to pass by 19th century physicists) and the all-pervasive 'odic force' of Baron von Reichenbach. The fundamental principle of magick that the doctrine of the astral light reaffirmed was 'all is one and one is all'–everything in the universe was intimately interconnected. Today we might imagine this astral light as the 'quantum vacuum', conceptualising it less as a substance (in the way that water is) but instead as a dimension or underlying quality of the universe (that gives rise to the probabilistic nature of events).

Levi's third principle, which was significantly developed by the adepts of the Hermetic Order of the Golden Dawn, concerned correspondences or 'like attracts like', what James Frazer went on to examine in *The Golden Bough* as 'sympathetic magic'. For Levi the doctrine of 'as above, so below' affirmed that what was within the macrocosm was reflected within the microcosm. Today models such as the holographic or fractal universe expound essentially the same doctrine. On the most superficial level one might say that humans are 'the magickal mirror of the universe' so that the constellation of Leo was related to the breast and the organ of the heart. However for Levi these chains of symbolic meaning were not to be taken strictly literally, rather it was the principle or quality that these symbols represented that would have a sympathy or connection. Thus the principle represented by the god Mars would correspond with activities such as conflict and qualities such as passion in the soul of the magician. It was this conception of the doctrine of correspondence that paved the way for the dream analysis of psychoanalysis and the archetypes of Carl Jung.

Following Levi, MacGregor Mathers and his brothers and sisters of the Golden Dawn successfully nurtured the growth of occultism as a corpus of knowledge. The schema of the Qabalah formed the primary skeleton upon which this body was fleshed out and works such as Crowley's *777* demonstrate how the muscles hang upon these bones. The Golden Dawn went on to expand the doctrine of correspondence to include Egyptian gods, Classical symbolism, Buddhist meditations and a formidable range of other categories to create an extensive and coherent system.

The adepts of the Golden Dawn built on Levi's work emphasising the principle of Imagination. They suggested that the Will was blind and impotent unless the Imagination had been sufficiently developed by practices such as visualisation and pathworking. The Will and Imagination were seen as the twin forces that accomplished magick. By furnishing the Imagination with the correct symbolic vocabulary, through knowledge of correspondences, mental images thus created could be given reality by the controlled use of the Will.

Added to the emphasis on Imagination we might add a fifth principle which was summed up nicely by Aleister Crowley as the fact that the Will (or Will framed by the Imagination) had to operate 'without lust of result'. For a magickal operation to be successful the magician had to be able to maintain a position of 'disinterested interest'. The sorcerer should be able to deliberately forget, or at least become consciously detached from, the outcome of the rite. In Austin Spare's system of magick various psychological devices were used to help the magician forget their desire. To use the psychoanalytic language that Spare favoured, the intention of the spell sinks down into the depths of the subconscious to do its work only if it remains undisturbed by conscious attention.

Spare was also notable in that his system of magick did not rely on elaborate paraphernalia. Indeed most of Spare's magickal work was conducted in everyday circumstances with nothing more than paper and pen. Magick had become increasingly 'all in the mind'. The highly personal and pared down style of Spare's sorcery exemplified the simple but effective occult technology that characterises modern magick. This was a move towards what has become known as 'open handed magick'.

It was during the 1970s, with the second phase of the modern occult revival in full swing, that the depth and range of esoteric systems appearing in the West made it increasingly hard to justify using only one approach (such as the Qabalah based iconography of post-Golden Dawn magick). The increasing amount of information emerging about Eastern occultism as well as new scientific developments (for instance in parapsychology) led researchers to propose another two key magickal principles. The contribution of these additional principles was closely linked to the emergence of the chaos magick current, they were:

Belief shifting - The method of the operation (ie magickal work) is not as important as one's firm belief in its efficacy. Belief shifting was a principle that was particularly in tune with the emergence of post-modernist philosophy into mainstream culture (in the 1980s). The focus on belief shifting derived from the observation that magickal power did not seem to be dependent on knowing arcane esoteric formulae, nor was it determined by whether you had access to paraphernalia constructed according to ancient prescription. Belief (and the ability to adopt different beliefs) seemed to be the thing that combined Will and Imagination and framed the space in which magick could take place.

Gnosis - The operation should be conducted in an altered state of consciousness. Whether through biofeedback, dance, sex, psychedelics or any number of other methods, entering a 'trance' state appeared to be a key element in successful magick. Today generating and successfully managing various states of gnosis is seen as pivotal to the pursuit of any magickal practice.

In addition to these new principles, movements such as Wicca had begun to fuse the 'high magick' of the ceremonial magician with the 'low' or 'natural' magick of the folk tradition. This vital union served to encourage the emerging tendency of magicians to go for simple and dramatic practices over complex formulaic rituals (William Gray's *The Rollright Ritual* is an example of a text that exists at the intersection of Golden Dawn style ceremony and modern neo-Pagan ritual). Western magick increasingly moved away from the Judeo-Christian/Masonic tradition and towards a wider neo-Pagan/Shamanic style.

A more general addition to the corpus of magick also came from what we might now recognise as the 'chaoist school'. This was to approach magick directly using 'the method of science' (as Crowley had hoped to do). Thus occultism was interpreted strongly in terms of producing verifiable results. A decision as to what magick might be profitably undertaken was conceptualised in terms of a probability model of the universe. This interpretation of the magickal universe drew strongly on the popularised language of quantum physics and, later, complex non-linear dynamics ('chaos mathematics'). The weird and distinctly occult universe explored by writers such as Fritjof Capra (in *The Tao of Physics*) seemed to provide just the right mixture of science and spirituality, which could provide a highly modern magickal vocabulary. Attempts were made to frame magick in terms of a materialist worldview (notably by Ramsey Dukes). Latterly the cyberpunk and information culture has also been pressed into the service of the occult to provide a different terminology apparently devoid of religious overtones (though this can be easily contested – see Erik Davis *TechGnosis*).

This 'technocratic' approach would have been a sad reduction of the scope and richness of the occult tradition were it not for the fact that the chaoist school also drew from the Discordian tradition. Inspired by the idea that if the science didn't work then perhaps the 'damned foolishness' would! Just as the psychedelic movement in '60s America had two sides (Leary – the cerebral eastern guru and Kesey – the crazed merry prankster) so chaos magick, through its key decade (the 1980s), maintained a deliberate lunacy alongside its assumed rationalism. The practice of banishing chaos rituals with laughter can be seen as emblematic of this. After a bunch of grown men and women have spent an hour waving their hands about, locked in a basement in Leeds, high on drugs and (apparently) convinced they are changing themselves and the wider universe through hidden powers – there is nothing left to do but laugh!

Although supposedly open to all influences and styles, chaos magick in the 1980s soon came to represent a definite type of sorcerer. Subscribers to journals such as *Chaos International* could be stereotyped as leather jacket wearing, rune carving dope heads who felt honour-bound to wage a war of 'we're more hardcore than you are' with all comers (but especially Thelemites). Fortunately such stereotypes were just that, empty images, and in fact many chaos magicians actively worked with colleagues from other traditions on projects that took them outside of their own sphere. (One of the most notable being the successful defence of the ancient woodland of Oxleas in central London against the threat of built development.)

The chaos magick system rests upon a paradox. Namely that the system claims that 'nothing is true' and yet itself emerges from the 19th century attempt to create a grand theory of magick. James Frazer attempted to demonstrate that the diverse religions of the world share the same set of symbols, and Marx attempted to show that all cultures move through the same socio-political processes. Freud and Jung proposed a common language of the unconscious that lay beneath apparent differences in language or culture. So Levi and the scholars of the Golden Dawn likewise proposed a similar universalism in magick. Chaos magick continued this idea; arguing that all occult systems are ultimately grounded in belief and gnosis and yet, in its more extreme manifestations, placed all 'reality' in subjective experience.

The paradox is also evident in the tension between the concept of the self found in some chaos magick texts (eg Carroll's *Psybermagick*) where 'selves' are admitted to but no unitary being is acknowledged. Yet at the same time much chaos sorcery is devoted to 'getting what you want' where the question of who the 'you' is that 'wants' is rarely examined. But these internal tensions or contradictions do not mean that chaos magick is not worthy of study. Indeed they may well imply just the differences and inconsistencies that one would expect to see in a rich and living tradition. Certainly the few key texts of chaos magick would prove valuable additions to the library of any occultist, whatever their preferred style of magick.

Today people who profess an interest in chaos magick wildly and happily incorporate a number of different magickal practices, technologies, and styles into their work. Indeed so wide is the appeal of this recension of the occult tradition, and the two principles that it has added to modern magickal praxis so commonplace, that today there is little value in considering chaos magick as a style of occultism in and of itself. Even those magicians who have a definite religious belief (be it Thelemic, Pagan or of some other type) often talk in terms of 'magickal paradigms'. Most occultists are reconciled to the idea that many of their most cherished sets of symbols and practices may well only be methods of 'slight of mind'. On the other hand many self-proclaimed chaos magicians have plunged deeper into one or more particular belief systems. Thus today a chaos magician is likely to be deeply involved in just a few traditions but with a working knowledge of many. Moreover the drive for 'change for change's sake' seems to have petered out, 'depth and diversity' seems to be the predominant approach rather than 'polymorphous paradigms plus a few key principles'.

So with this book we can confidently announce the death of chaos magick. If we want in the future to delineate highly eclectic approaches to magick from those that are bounded within a given tradition or system perhaps the word 'freestyle' might be appropriate. Perhaps the chaos current has done its job in freeing occultism from the dead grip of religion and other superstition. Thus we might simply talk about 'magick' and only prefix the word when we want to discuss a particular style within it (eg 'Thelemic magick', 'voudou magick', 'mimetic magick' and so on). In the same way we talk about 'art' and then define different media or styles – neo-classical art, surrealist art, visual art, etc.

The meta-belief that 'Nothing is True, Everything is permitted' and the eight-rayed star of chaos can stand guard, ensuring that magick does not become swallowed up by the beasts of rationalist technology, new age religion or Paganism. Groups such as The Illuminates of Thanateros and itinerant chaoists will remain as the agent provocateurs of esoteric culture, chipping away at any limits that others might seek to impose on the magickal discourse. Equally chaos magicians will remain those gallant souls who battle the demons of delusion, acknowledging that it is certainly important to do 'what feels right' but always asking that awkward question 'yes, but did it work?'

Chaos is Dead! Long Live Magick!

# Thou, who art I, Beyond all I Am

I am kneeling before an image of Mama Yemanja – the goddess of salt water, the goddess of the sea. Here is an image of a woman in a full blue skirt, holding a silver mirror. She is a clay figurine, bought in Lisbon, shipped there from Brazil. Thus the goddess of the sea has crossed the ocean. First with those terrible slave ships from Yorubaland to the New World, and then back again to Europe, and finally to my windowsill altar in Brighton. Here am I, a white man, kneeling before the black mother of the oceans. But it is not Mama Yemaja that I want to speak of here, but the god that comes before all Orisha, the god that led me to the black sea mother – Ori.

The Ori is the head, that part of us that comes into the world first. At one level Ori is the skull, the physical fact of the cranium, the organic reality of the brain as the container or transceiver for the mind. The Ori leads us through the market place of the world, through our trials and tribulations and helps us bear our load in life. The Ori is the guide, the one star in sight. The Ori is destiny, the omega point. Ori is astrological Pluto the outermost limit, it is the atomic son of the sun – Ori is death. Ori is the assurance of a good death – a death that is the fulfilment of life, a fulfilment of desire not a tragic postscript to life. Ori is an end that is something good, something fabulous, ecstatic, and righteous.

I am starting this work with Ori because Ori comes first and Ori bears the load. I am starting this work with Ori. Ori you are first and last. Ori, this text is your invocation, your hymn of praise. To speak aloud these words with intent is your ritual:

> Ori the master of all.
> It is Ori we should praise.
> The rest of the body comes to naught
> When Ori is missing from the body.
> What remains is useless.
> What remains is incapable of carrying any load.
> It is Ori which bears the load.
> Ori, I pray you.
> Do not desert me,
> You, the Lord of all things.

The dogs Ori helps it to cut through the bush.
Thunder uses Ori to split the Iroko tree.
Every deer grows a pair of horns  through Ori.
With its Ori, fish swims without mishap in water.
Owawa, Rats Ori helps it to go through caves.
Ori precedes man,
It also guides him,
Ori plans good things for its owner.
It is Ori alone
Who can accompany his devotee to any place
Without turning back
If I have money,
It is my Ori I will  praise
It is my Ori to whom I will give praise
My Ori, it is you
All good things I have on earth,
It is my Ori, I will praise.
My Ori, it is you.
No God shall offer protection
Without sanction from Ori
Ori, we salute you
Whose protection precedes that of any other Orisha.
Without sanction from Ori,
Ori, we salute you
Ori that is destined to live
Whosoever sacrifice Ori choose to accept,
Let him rejoice.
Ori the actor, the stalwart divinity
One who guides one to wealth, gives one riches.
Ori, the beloved, governor of all the divinities.
Ori, who takes one to the good place.
Ori, behold the good place and accompany me thereto.
There is no divinity like Ori,
One's Ori is one's providence.
My Ori, lead me home
My Ori, lead me home
Ori, the most concerned
My skull, the most concerned in sacrificial rites.
Ori, I thank you.
Ori, I thank you for my destiny.
My skull, I thank you for my destiny.

Ori, I thank you.
Character, character
It is character that overtakes
Man's conduct
When he get to heaven,
Keep your character.
Everything is in the hands of Ori,
Ori is everything
Ori is good
What is left is Iwa
The one who performs actions is one whose Ori exists.
Fate is man's endowment.
May my Ori accompany me home.
I am here on a journey.
The world is a market place, heaven is home.
My Ori, behold the good place
And take me there.
Bad Ori is not mine.
Good Ori, that is mine.
Good Ori does not engage in business and end up in debt.
Good Ori does not suffer in the world.
Good Ori does not languish before it becomes prosperous.
Good Ori, that is mine.
If you want to have money
Inquire of your head.
If you want to start trading,
Inquire of your head first;
If you want to build a house,
Inquire of your head.
If you want to take a wife
Inquire of your head first.
Head, please do not shut the gate
It is to you I am coming.
Come and make my life prosperous.
My fate is from Olorun
Man created into this world cannot change my endowment
My creator, I beseech you
My creator, place me above the world.
That which one chooses on bended knees
Is what one finds in the world
One's endowment

Is one's fate
Operere…Operere..it is where I choose my Ori,
My Ori, that is where the enemy cannot know.
One's Ori is one's saviour.
The god that saves one like one's Ori does not exist.
Where I chose my Ori, my Ori, that is where the enemy cannot
know
A big leaf will not sprout a little leaf.
Enemy of the open, watch out
Enemy of the darkness, take care.
Only Ori knows where my feet are going…
I shall reach where I am going….
A big leaf will not sprout a little leaf.

The first steps are always difficult, dislocated, shaky. This is not wrong, this only means that the journey is a new one. By these tentative steps is the journey begun.[1]

The space is made ready for your prayer the Ori Oriki. Words are spoken, signs are made. A candle is lit, incense of frankincense is used.

The technique using the Oriki is to recite the prayer once, briskly, breathing fast and shallow, high up in the body. The prayer is given under one's breath. Then the prayer is repeated more slowly, and louder, this time with the breath going deeper into the body. The prayer is repeated again very slowly, with deep long breaths and more loudly. This third stage represents a descent into the territory of the Ori, into a deep devotional trance.

The Oriki can be repeated slowly as many times as required at this point to stay within the meditative state. When ready the process is reversed and the Oriki is repeated more quickly, moving the breath up, and again at a faster pace until one is out of the trance. At that point divination can be productively done, asking Ori for guidance. Ori will always give the best advice.

Ori you are always there, always with me, always leading me on. You are there for everyone, whosoever looks for you will find you. You are the Holy Guardian Angel. You can make all aspects of the self pull together, you provide coherence, alignment. You can twist the threads of the unconscious, the consciousness, the ego and the superconscious into a single cord. You help all the aspects of the self pull together as one.

Ori, you can appear as an angel, you can appear as an animal totem, you can appear as a fleshless skull.

Your oil is made of jasmine, sandalwood and rose, your incense is Abra-Melin – thick with the heady perfume of storax. Olibanium is the crown of your odours.

Ori, I confess to you, I confess my fear of being. My terrors, childish and adult, my fears of the World. From you I understand that the universe does care – that your love is the love of the universe for that which is within it, a pervasive Self-Love. Through you I know that love is a reality, not only as a moral force, but also as a tangible substrate of creation. Gravity is the love of mass for mass, love is as ubiquitous as the curvature of space. Your existence persuades me of the reality of the love of the Other.

I long for you! I yearn for you! Like a child for the breast, like the lover for the beloved! Through you I come to know the true bhakti yoga!

I come to you, after weeks of preparation, of earnestly entreating you through daily prayer, through repetitions of the Ori Oriki. I come to you in a triad of candles, making a three-sided pyramid, a vessel for the primary invocation of Self by Self. I am within your demon triangle! You are my holy demon!

Before me, one light placed in a cauldron, set upon this, leaning against the wall, a voodoo skull mask, the physical, slightly cartoon-grotesque representation of my own skull, my Ori.

To begin with I employ tobacco and cannabis pollen, keeping the purpose of the work in mind. I stand and dance, letting my body, letting the chi, loosen and flow. Letting my mind build up the three-sided pyramid in which I stand. The feeling in your temple is of light, yellow, solar fire and expansion.

I stand in the form of the cross and intone the sonics IAO – the formula of the dying and resurrected god.[2]

22

I began by reciting the Ori Oriki, the first time I have done this fully from memory. I let my awareness flit between the sense of the shape I am building up on the astral (a yellow three-sided pyramid), the longing for you, my Holy Guardian Angel, and the focus of the words in the Oriki.

I inflame myself with prayer!

> A cross shining into the sun,
> The golden glow of aeons flown
> The passing of this life, an easy road.
> Where unseen hands guide the wisest heart,
> An angelic ministry from eternal Other called,
> To smile and care and offer succour.
> Serpent rear upon your star!
> Kia bend your lambent kiss!
> Headless one, my head, my skull!
> Omega point of my death!
> Gather me up because I'm lost!
> And know that with you I am found,
> By all creation.
> I love you,
> I yearn for you.
> Ori, Holy Guardian Angel,
> who is always with me -
> Hear my prayer!

A prayer along these lines is spoken spontaneously, with great longing. With Great Longing!
I repeat the Oriki again, this time pulling the astral golden light of Tiphereth into the triangle. The light falls! It falls in great shafts of sun into the temple!

I repeated the Oriki again and take a hit of DMT and lay back. As the hit comes on I lie back, my arms outstretched to two of the points of the triangle, my feet pointing at the third. Thus I am a Tau cross within a triangle.

My body is composed of a million tiny angular fragments of gold which are swept up towards the light at the apex of the pyramid. I feel the barriers between myself and you, my Holy Guardian Angel, breaking down.

I decide to snort a line of ketamine. As I feel the drug begin to come on I lay again in the Tau cross position I am frightened and pursue the fear to it's root – 'all fear is fear of letting go'. In that sense Buddha was right! I grip my wand and feel myself sinking into the K-hole. As I do so I say the Oriki until the point where consciousness fades out, everything is distant, the limits of my body changing, morphing.

Ori I die into you! I dedicate the extinguishing of my consciousness to you!

Then I awake and I see the light. As clear as day, over the voodoo skull mask golden filaments of light falling down, like angel hair - into the cauldron, onto my body.

In a flash I know your name (or perhaps one name) my beloved Holy Guardian Angel! A name that I had first used when I was 14 years old and just starting out in ritual magick! And now my Ori reveals itself as the being that I had first encountered over 19 years ago. Of course, my angel was with me all along!

I recite the Oriki again – feeling powerful and certain and centred in a way that stretches right down to the depths of my being.

Standing in a cruciform stance I intone ORI and IAO, thrice each. ORI bringing the energy from the earth (O), through the solar/heart/resh (R) to the crown (I). IAO, earthing the energy once again. The connection is established.

I laugh with joy!
It is done! Ω AUM!

As the Beast sayeth:

> Thou, who art I, beyond all I am,
> Who hast no nature and no name,
> Who art, when all but Thou are gone,
> Thou, centre and secret of the Sun,
> Thou, hidden spring of all things known
> And unknown, Thou aloof, alone,

Thou, the true fire within the reed
Brooding and breeding, source and seed
Of life, love, liberty, and light,
Thou beyond speech and beyond sight,
Thee I invoke, my faint fresh fire
Kindling as mine intents aspire.
Thee I invoke, abiding one,
Thee, centre and secret of the Sun,
And that most holy mystery
Of which the vehicle am I!

I am given your sigil, your sigil is Ω - the letters O, R, I are in it. Your promise of a good death is held there! Perhaps I will spray paint tags of your symbol around the town in praise!

After this comes the dry phase - as it must. The time when concentration is hard, when nothing seems enough to quiet the mind. When all that can be done is to keep going, this is the time when devotion is really measured. First the tentative steps, then the easy strides as the Oriki is bedded down in memory and then the halting, stuttering, as though the mind is manacled. In any practice there is this low ebb, it is hard but welcomed as a mark of progress.

Yet in this time a possibility begins to emerge (though this can only be seen in hindsight). From dreams and strange longings arises a form, which calls out to be made. A golden cross, and on that cross a heart, and within that heart an open eye. (Later I would manufacture this cross and charge it with power.)

But the abyss is wide. Sometimes the Oriki produces tiredness, it is hard to go on. Sometimes waves of tiredness sweep upon me, it would be easy to stop, to claim that the work of the day has fatigued me beyond endurance. But I have made a commitment and devotion is the watchword of this practice – on! On!

Sometimes the Oriki provokes movements, involuntarily, in the body, rolling of the head, making the shape of the omega sign with the hands, flicking ones hands, clapping, rocking. Often I must bow my head and open up the spot between my shoulders. Often my prayer takes chanting, moving form with hands clasped together and wrung in earnest devotion.

Then one night the Oriki is strange. Perhaps it is a fault in my poor preparation of the temple that night, perhaps this is a message to pay more attention to the Eshu, to Elegba.[3] The animals in the house mew, and hiss, the corners are full of shadows, of spirits. A paranormal pawl is over the house. There are the beginnings of strange sensations, clear physical stirrings in my spine, clear physical stirrings.

But the Ori is the guide, and the Oriki is the path. I hold fast and clearly banish. Has it been a test? A side effect? A message from the Eshu spirits?

As the darkness is driven away with food and music and time so understanding of the beauty of it dawns. Ori is the heart as well as the head, it is Tiphereth of the Tree of Life. Tiphereth is the son of the Sun, the deliverer, and the redeemer. Tiphereth is the guide, the Holy Guardian Angel. So these dark spirits are the shadow of the sun. They are the nighside sun, the Qlipoth. As the Adept invokes the Holy Guardian Angel so they must begin the work of summoning their demons. For Abra-Melin knowledge and conversation leads to the binding of the denizens of Hell. For me the work of the Ori leads to a need to know the Eshu, to pay respect and to gain good relations with the spirits of the crossroads and of the crossing places. If the flame of devotion is not to blind one into believing that the universe is all selfless love then it must be balanced with the shadow of the Eshu.[4]

Ori I praise you! I praise you!

When I visit Glastonbury I call your Oriki into the wind from the summit of the Tor. When I am waiting in line at the market I mutter your hymn of praise. I clean my heart with love of you and this only makes it bigger. I am more full of love and more able to love, I have more to give and more joy.
Ori you give me wisdom that I rush to record after each devotion. You show me how the head is a nexus of possibilities.[5] Lines or tubes, each a thread in The Pattern of being, each a discourse, a strand in the web of wyrd – these all intersect within the head. Each head is a place of intention, though it is itself brought into being by these threads, so it can change them. You give me a

vision of the skull, connected by these lines of possibility, these lines of intention to all things in the universe.

Often I perform the Oriki with a single flame before me, sat in front of my magickal mirror. Before me are cast two shadows. Sometimes you reveal yourself in these shadows. These shadow heads, shaped like omega signs, become strangely three-dimensional. I can see within them features, I can see within them electric blue veins, organs, alchemical processes taking place. The organic forms of nature have given rise to mind. Certain conditions and interactions of molecules have created electrical pulses and radiance. These become thought and create a new universe of being. I wonder at your power Ori, my skull.

Sometimes in the mirror I watch the surface of my face. Sometimes I see the age creeping into me, sometimes I see the form of my power animal flicker through my features. I see my expression, the outward form, how this changes, how everything changes. I begin to see ageing as a process of being led by you home, towards a good death, towards the fulfilment of the desire to live.
I see this now so clearly when nature reveals that I have helped create a new life.[6]

There are stirrings of energy in my body; up and down my spine like itches or tiny pinpricks. By invoking you, my Ori, my head, I have begun to summon the goddess at the root of all things. I will put your sigil in the fetish within the temple dedicated to Her.[7]

Ori always brings good advice. Ori helps me to use the healing cross. Ori teaches a technique that involves holding the cross and breathing golden energy from the crown, down the spine and out through the heart chakra and into the patient. In this way a dear friend is saved.[8]

Ori comes to me and guides me in an ayahuasca ritual where I think I am dying. Ori holds me and guides me and reminds me to summon the help of the Eshu spirits. They help me make the transition. Ayahuasca brings me a vision of a great black goddess, proud and erotic. She wears a leopard pelt, and has bright parrot feathers woven into her matted locks. She is Kali, she is the spirit of the slaves in Peru. She bends over and begins to shit, she shits out all my sin. She shits in my face all the mistakes I have ever made, all my failings, all my wrongdoings. I go through this darkness, this loathsome horror, Eshu helps me and Ori leads me on. I take heed of what I can do to change things, and go through the mourning process for those acts that cannot be redeemed.

Then in the darkness of the ayahuasca vision Ori comes as an eagle and scoops out my abdomen. Ori scoops out my guts and lights a fire beneath my ribs. In the cage of my skeleton a fire is built and the eagle becomes a phoenix and I rise, I rise, I rise!

I feel the bones of my skull, like tectonic plates grind and change position. I feel the vibrations of the shamanic brew shift the knots and blockages of energy in my body. Opening me up like a doorway.

Ori you are with me. I have worshipped you, I have met you in devotional stillness and psychedelic trance. I have taken your name and acknowledged you as my destiny. You have revealed the master of my head[9], you have opened the door to the magick of Spiritism, Candomblé, Macumba, Voudou, Yoruba and many more paths.

Now the months of undertaking your Oriki as a daily duty are over. You have guided me through this difficult and rewarding work and you remain a star for me navigate by, through the marketplace of the world, to my home in heaven. You are automatically invoked before every divination and never cease to give perfect and clear results.

Ori the last day of your working comes, but this is not the end of my devotions to you. Instead I shall pray everyday in my heart and remember to invoke you at my death. The final night of the Oriki is one in which your gentle yellow rays bathe me in bliss. I see you face as a horned countenance, a triangle, a golden thread linking all sentience and all moments of consciousness.

Sweeter than honey, more gentle than velvet, more comforting than my mothers lap, you care for me! You flow through and intoxicate me like an intelligent wine; you show the way like a shining path!

It is Ori we should praise!

# Models of the Ori/Holy Guardian Angel – what is it?

The text above represents a distillation of 3 months worth of magickal work. This comprised a daily recitation of the Ori Oriki. On some occasions this meant a prayer when circumstances dictated, on others a more formal ritual (using a technique such as the Gnostic Pentagram Ritual to open and close) was used. The ritual described above involving DMT and Ketamine took one whole evening. The ayahuasca ritual was not specifically concerned with the Ori work but took place towards the end of the Ori working. The ayahuasca rite itself was a 'concentration' (ie remaining silent and still, having taken the drug).

I am greatly indebted to Brother Kondwani 23 for supplying me with the Ori Oriki text, the technique for its use and his valuable support in exploring this territory.

In the Western African traditions, as well as the 'hybrid' systems such as the Afro-Brazilian Macumba, the same idea is maintained in the concept of the Ori. The Ori is one's providence, one's fate, and one's saviour. In the Ori Oriki Ori takes centre stage in the belief system, at times seeming to be highly personal and concrete (the Ori is identified with the head or skull). In other lines the Oriki Ori sounds more like 'The Force' as 'Thunder uses Ori to split the Iroko tree'. The Holy Guardian Angel (HGA) as Ori, is in a sense identical with the True Will, the individual thread of the wyrd on which the separating 'ego I' consciousness coagulates.

The HGA, the Ori, is the skull, that which comes first into the world, that transceiver for consciousness, the 'two and a half pounds of electrified fat' that serve to amplify the 'random' mutterings of Kia into manifest, structured existence.

Using the terminology of Lacanian psychoanalysis the HGA could be interpreted as the perfect 'ego ideal'. An ego ideal is the internalised gaze(s) through which we imagine that our actions are perceived.

When we do something, anything, we imagine not only why we are doing it (what we are striving to be) but also from where we are being watched.

Listen to children, notice how they need to be observed, 'look at me mum', until they begin to internalise a set of ego-ideals – mental constructs about who is watching them - that they can then use without needing a physical human gazing on. Imagine doing something rebellious or nasty, or indeed an act of self-less kindness. Somewhere in your thoughts about that act (according to Lacan) is an ego-ideal, a person who you imagine watching you. As you smash a window in the school maybe you imagine the leader of the gang looking proudly on as you do the deed. Maybe as you nurse your partner you imagine your mother looking approvingly at your altruism. When we do any act it is important to understand not just what we are trying to be by the act (a rebel or a carer) but also from where we imagine ourselves being seen. The HGA, according to this model, could be a notional 'perfected self as ego-ideal', you as the 'Great Wise Magus'. As well as acting 'in the gaze of' the ego-ideal, the effect of that gaze (obviously) modifies one's actions. Thus the internalised idea of the HGA (ego-ideal) drives us towards 'spiritual perfection', or, if you prefer, 'magickal excellence'.

The apparent moralism and religious overtones of the HGA can, of course, put people off. As Phil Hine points out, even the name Holy Guardian Angel sounds pretty pompous. Even if the term 'Augoides' or 'genius' are employed in this working the techniques that are recommended for Knowledge and Conversation are still very much of the devotional sort. But for me, going beyond the 'yuck – angels! Worship – pah!' factor is a key issue.

The HGA is Julian Cope being able to say (in his album *Jehovahkill*) 'I'm not afraid of the cross'. It is engaging with the Christian, monotheist traditions, getting the value out of them and going beyond that adolescent rebellion against them. (Not that contact with your HGA means you can't still have fun doing Black Masses.) This is religion on one's own terms, but it is also about humility and being receptive rather than just stamping round the circle being the All Powerful Adept.

In some respects, the HGA is akin to a shamanic power animal, though I agree with Phil Hine, not in the way the thing feels. Certainly the HGA may take on animal forms, but often one of the key features of the HGA is its formlessness. Aiwaz for Crowley was a shadowy, proud figure, dressed in middle eastern robes and with a darkness before his eyes. The HGA may well have a name, possibly a sigil or seal but rarely a fixed, complex form (as a servitor might).

The HGA may be thought of as a more 'internal' entity than many the magician might encounter. But either way the HGA (usually) knows a lot more than we do; it is the Cray supercomputer of superconsciousness to the pocket calculator of conscious awareness. (And this, of course, is a big part of the reason behind wanting to establish a rapport with it.)

What is also key about the desire to obtain Knowledge and Conversation is the notion that the universe is not simply blind forces but that 'the Other' cares for us. The philosophical basis of this idea is complex but a concrete example of its use is this. In the belief system of Alcoholics Anonymous people who want to give up the booze need to look outside themselves and seek the aid of a 'higher power' in order to support them in not drinking. The 'higher power' has to care that the individual is killing themselves with drink and want to help. The Universe as a whole, or the prime mover of reality (God), is seen to give a damn and actively want to help the alcoholic.

Whether you want to explore the metaphysics of a caring universe or simply consider it a handy paradigm (or both) it does not seem to matter as long as you are sincere! (As an aside rarely is God, 'Olorun', addressed by African ritual since he/it is seen as so distant from humanity that he/it has little interest in us. However in the Ori Oriki, Olorun is addressed directly because the power of the Ori forms a connection with the rarefied divine.) The point is that the Knowledge and Conversation represents an opportunity to experience the reality that 'God is Love', and that God (the Kosmos) does care for every atom of creation.

The HGA is 'myself made perfect' (complete, undivided - as it says in the Bornless Ritual). I consider that the HGA is myself as the eschatology of the ego - as the self at the moment of death. This is when we are 'perfect' in the sense that subject and object collapse, as far as our individual awareness is concerned, forever.

We are all pulled, in our chariots of history, to the strange attractor of our death. I believe this personal eschaton contains within it the possibility of such a 'perfect death'. By which I mean being able to meet the moment of death with equanimity and enjoy a peak, numinous experience (which, since there is no conscious 'after', subjectively lasts forever). An eternal joyous moment outside the circles of time is created in the fraction of a second before the brain is starved completely of oxygen and stops working. In this way the HGA is like the Castenada notion of death, always at one's shoulder and not to be feared. Death guides us all because it is the end of the road for consciousness – to have a good death, to make an ally of death is indeed a powerful magick.

The HGA is also Our Future Selves, N' Aton (in the Maatian cosmology). The ever-coming one.
The HGA is Tiphereth – the golden glow descending upon the mind, even as the body is split into a thousand tiny fragments - painlessly dissolved into the great Resh of the solar Logos.
The HGA is the frame in which the dance of the IAO formula takes place. Where –

I, the Yod the seed pours out in eternal possibility of the one brilliance.
A, is the open-hearted wounding of being-in-time, the abyss and the travail of the world.
O, is the universe of being, the eye of A'yin. The universe as a need for spiritual perfection, as a playing field in which consciousness must give birth to all possible forms. It is the secret generative eye and the base of the witches cone of power. The circle in which we are spellbound. O is also the Devil/ Pan

The HGA is the beloved – something that we yearn to be with (and that yearns to be with us) and yet is not us. This separation gives rise to the HGA and to the mechanism by which we seek to make the return journey – love.

As the flower loves the sun and so turns to face it, so the magician turns towards the HGA.

The term Iwa (used in the Oriki) means character. One of the aims of Yoruba spiritual practice is for the individual to get Iwa-pele 'cool' or good character. An insight that Ori gave me in this work is how magick is the process of exploring and developing the vehicle of the self so that it can move without resistance along the path of the Ori. The pictorial image is of a shuttle moving on a loom, the thread is the path of the True Will, and the road that Ori leads us along. The shuttle is the vehicle (one's character). By having a 'cool' character we are better placed to enjoy life, to meet its challenges and to follow the path of the True Will without balking at those things that are difficult or trying to 'push the river'. Ori may be seen as one's consciousness and Iwa as one's behaviour. In other words the more one is consciously in tune with 'the divine', the more one's day-to-day behaviour should reflect this.

By their fruits shall ye know them.

# Fotamecus Film Majik

Clock watching - the hands of the timepiece are the bars of our self-imposed prison. Time is always running out, running out the door as the bell goes. Time is money, and money talks, time structures and strictures. It marks and it moves, it is omnipresent as God and as inscrutable as the night.

Clocks, symbols of that ancient god Chronos, cut time up. They slice the continuum of time into segments that wither like the coils of a dying earthworm. Chronos, the clock, the measurer who takes our endless dreaming and breaks it into discrete units. The regular ticking of the clock, the external, the strictly determined period. Chronos demands an objective reality of time. Chronos demands a shared notion of time, his will was made possible by the railways and now, thanks to the microsecond exactitude of information systems, his domination is global.

Time no longer flows like the river. Instead it is rigidly channelled, suffocated like the sickly industrial canal. It is hemmed about with atomic clocks, and clock cards and hourly totals.

Yet we all know the truth, we all sense that this objective measure of time is only one feather on the Great Arrow, passing from past to future.

There is the past of memory, slipping and morphing in the mind, outside of notions of objective recording, the past re-members itself continually and changes as easily as the shape of smoke in the wind.

In the mediations of yogis and in the ecstatic peaks of drug intoxicated wisdom, time stands still. There is no past, no future, not even any now. There is, for example, a part of me that is still sitting on the Isles of Scilly with my lover, looking towards the horizon and feeling my LSD immersed consciousness spreading out across the whole globe, occupying the immense space where the sky and sea meet. There was no time then in that numinous eternal moment - I am still there (for dreaming is only called such after we awaken).

The future. Hurtling towards us with the velocity of the impossible instant. Possibility guided by the probability and chains of causality that we recognise. But time can crawl too, as it did in the later years of the second millennium. Time flies when you're having fun. Suddenly the lights go up and they call time. You look around at the grinning faces of the night-club and time slows right down.

It is this subjective component of time that Chronos stands against. The rigid ticking of his clock, the immutable unit of the hour, the suffocating limit of the exact second.

Chronos - your time has come!

# Keyman Speaks:

Indifference Productions
FOTAMECUS PROJECT
Project outline and history

The purpose of the project is to make a film as a magickal experiment, specifically, as an attempt to invoke the 'egregore' of Fotamecus. Fotamecus is a thought form or servitor created by a magician through the means of a sigil. The basic mythology surrounding the form of Fotamecus is still new and open to development but I have taken the specific name from the workings written up by Fenwick Rysen…In essence Fotamecus has the power to manipulate time by compressing and expanding it. In this role Fotamecus represents a power of time that is in conflict with the established and existing order of time given by Chronos, whose talisman is the clock face. Fotamecus is not simply a 'non-linear' time, but a chaotic time. Instead of the metronomic beat of time we will find the 'duration' of time (as suggested, for example, by the philosopher Henri Bergson). Time is not a series of moments set before and after the present, as though in a cinematic roll of film where each frame represents a $25^{th}$ of a second, it is instead the duration of an event, as in the time it takes sugar to dissolve in water, the time of waiting.

The aim of the project, originally, was for me to attempt to make the film myself with my own magickal background, using actors and friends for the parts. As I thought more about the project it felt right to attempt, at least initially, to see if the project could be a collective group work rather than a more solitary operation through which a visually experimental piece would be made. The advantage of the group work would be that it would increase the blur between the 'film' side of the project and the 'magick' since the film would take on a slightly more recognisable form for a wider audience. It would be slightly less visually experimental in order to become more practically experimental. The goal of the project from the beginning was to attempt a process of participation where, with their implicit consent, the audience 'takes part' in the invocation through their experience of watching the film. Such a participate operation firstly implies consent, which would be done at the start of the film, and then suggests a greater use of narrative structure in order to let the audience slip into the willing suspension of disbelief. The use of a semi-documentary style 'recording' of a rite seemed the ideal genre vehicle in this instance. To this end I have approached a number of magicians and pagans, including locally in Brighton as well as on email lists through which a meeting took place with someone from London. I have also discussed the possibility of a Brighton based animator and pagan being involved in the project at both a design level and at an animation level, allowing the film to integrate a small degree of animated effect work which will enable the thought form to be visually suggested to the audience with greater impact. This animated aspect of the film is intended to be abstract and free, a black scratch of colour and movement rather than a determined form. Think of the shapes that you can see on the insides of your eyelids with your eyes shut and the light on.

I first heard about the Fotamecus project from a fellow sorcerer in the IOT. I was in London participating in a meeting of one of the temples there. The Sister I got talking to (as we changed out of our civilian clothes and into robes) began to tell me that she had been approached by Keyman, via email, with a view to taking part in the film project. She was aware that I lived in Brighton and said she'd pass on my address.

Keyman subsequently got in touch and we met up in a pub. We talked and it became obvious that we shared a number of similar ideas and would certainly be able to work together. From the perspective of the Brighton chaos magick temple the whole thing sounded great. After all it's not often that you get somebody offering to make you the stars of a magickal film, provide you with specially made robes and generally give you the chance to use professional filmmaking techniques as the medium through which to launch a sigil!

The story of Fotamecus begins in a crossing of the desert

## Fenwick Rysen speaks

27 June 1997
History
Fotamecus was originally a sigil created in spring of 1996 when I was showing the Mad Prophet some sigilization techniques. The Mad Prophet kept the paper used for the demonstration and began using it when he was driving, the sigil's intent being to "Force Time Into Compression." Ruben, a friend of both the Mad Prophet, and me was brought in on this, and two people began directing energy at it.

Fotamecus crossed the Sigil/Servitor line after both Ruben and the Mad Prophet attended a Metallica concert in Sacramento at which Quinn is said to have smiled evilly when looking at the crowd and muttered "Free gnosis..." before opening himself to channel and becoming a one-man-mosh. On the drive back, both Ruben and the Mad Prophet dumped the excess energy into Fotamecus and made it home in half the time it should have taken. I was informed and intrigued, and on the Death Valley Pilgrimage (three days in a van with seven chaos mages) Fotamecus was put to the test: The group directed a great amount of energy at him to help shorten the time to drive from Santa Rosa (north of San Francisco) to Death Valley.

On the first leg of the trip everyone looked at the clock before entering Vallejo. Fifteen minutes later we had travelled almost fifty miles, through the MacArthur Maze (the most dizzying interchange of highways known to man), in the Thanksgiving traffic. The second car with us, which we lost immediately, preceding this, had continued to drive undaunted behind us. They never stopped. We wasted 45 minutes in Livermore before getting back on the road and coincidentally running into them again.

There was only one side effect.

The last three exits on I-5 before Bakersfield, which should have taken us 15 minutes to pass, took closer to an hour. For time compressed, time was expanded. For us, expanded on perhaps one of the most boring stretches of highway in California. At this point, several of my friends and I sat down and did some work on Fotamecus, making him a viral servitor: He could spawn copies of himself. We wired these together into a network so that if one compresses time but doesn't want to expand it, it passes off the duty for expansion to another Fotamecus servitor in the network. They all work together and the more copies out there, the better it works.

This was the beginning. From a spontaneous sigil Fotamecus would become the 'viral servitor', and from this, through being interacted with, fed and cared for by a global conspiracy of magicians, it would grow. Growing to become an egregore, a 'group mind' being. Through the project initiated by Keyman, Fotamecus was seeking to become even more powerful, to develop from egregore to fully fledged godhood.

This was to be a wonderful opportunity, it's not everyday that you get to be the midwife to a new god and film the process to boot. Moreover the key weapon for the formation of Fotamecus the god would be the technology of the enemy, a clockwork 16mm camera. The division of time into discrete frames that makes film possible would be pressed into the service of Fotamecus. We would use the technology of Chronos against him!

The camera became a participant in the rituals. Sometimes it would be a passive, documentary being - recording, variously operated by different members of the group. Sometimes we would become actors, repeating actions and going through the motions, never exactly scripted but having at least some intention of what we wanted to be captured on film. Sometimes the camera would become the active eye/I in the ritual, another person, another view.

Our aim was to create the film, not as a passive viewing experience, but as a talismanic object. A portal through which the rituals that we worked would emerge onto the cinema screen. Our will was that the Fotamecus film would itself be the climax of the ritual, and that the creation of the movie would be a pivotal step in moving Fotamecus from egregore to god status. By watching the film (which would be one element in a larger performance event) one would be tapping in to the Fotamecus energy. Showing the film would allow the meme viral servitor to reproduce in the consciousness of the viewer. Moreover the viewer would be presented through the film itself with both the Fotamecus current as raw experience and also with a series of techniques for working with that current. Watching this film means participation not consumption.

Of course you have to be careful.

Ritual isn't the same as theatre, though both have much in common. Within theatre the actors are possessed by their characters to a greater or lesser degree, and we, the audience, are asked to suspend our disbelief and enter into the paradigm of the play. Magickal ritual is created and performed without an audience in mind. The viewer of the occult ceremony isn't a public that must be won over and disarmed by appealing performance. Rather the audience is the self, the conspiracy of selves that make up each of us. The aim is to be just convincing enough that the company of self will accept as true the reality of the ritual space. If there is another observer it is perhaps the discarnate forces one summons, the demons, the spirits, the gods who, by their very imaginal nature, are quite willing to enter into the spirit of the rite.

This is, in part, why rituals look so shit on film. For example:

*From the outside:* the woman walks forward and raises her hands, as though sleepwalking, in front of her. She looks by turns abstracted, as though confused, and tight lipped as though she is about to cry. She steps forward, flinging her hands outwards and down and says the word 'Nemo!' Nothing much seems to happen.

*From the inside:* after years of preparation Soror X prepares to emerge from the abyss and into her new place as Mistress of the Temple 8=3. Her mind focused with intensity, and yet calm as an icy pool, she gathers her resolve. The sacrament she has taken reaches a peak within her, before her the Garden of Souls awaits, she has crossed the desert of despair and battled with the demon Choronzon! Then, in a moment that lasts forever she rends the veil and claims her new title etc etc.

You see the problem.

But sometimes having not too much on the outside of a ritual can be helpful. As is often the case less is sometimes more. Take this ceremony by Fenwick, which appears as one element in the Fotamecus filmrite.

## Fenwick speaks:

Time Consumption
-or-
Yet Another Fotamecus Rite

*OBJECTIVE:*
*To draw the power of the Fotamecus time manipulation egregore into the participants and thus imbue them with the ability to distort time.*

*NOTES:*
*This isn't really a very structured ritual; it's mostly social in context with a short ritual-like component at*

*the very end. If it feels like you're not doing a ritual until about step -4, you're doing it right. This is probably because of the heavy kitchen-witchery style of most of this ritual.*

MATERIALS REQUIRED:
An oven
Sugar cookie dough (either ingredients for home-made or a supermarket pre-packaged dough)
A cookie sheet
A small clock for each participant
A Fotamecus Talisman (this can be paper drawn with the sigil or any physical object other than a mechanical timepiece)
A small magnet and glue (optional, necessary only if talisman is to become a refrigerator magnet)
Participants, one of whom is Head Cook (HC)

RITUAL:

-11   Participants gather, chat, socialise, and have fun. People should be entertaining themselves with food, conversation, games, etc. The central area around which this circulates should eventually move towards the kitchen.

-10   The participants start baking cookies. If you've got pre-pack cookie batter, this is as simple as slicing the cookies and tossing them on the tray. If you're baking from scratch, the HC should be in charge and ask people to measure and mix things for him/her, trying to get everyone involved.

-9    Once you have one cookie on the tray for each participant, everyone should gather and simultaneously impress their clocks into their cookies while saying "Praise unto Fotamecus! Chronos, your time has come!".

-8    Put ze cookiez in ze oven an' bake 'em.

-7    Socialise some more; have fun. Play a game of Twister. Put a Monty Python movie on for atmosphere. Get some shinai and spar in the back yard. Engage in meaningless ontological debate. You get the general idea.

-6    Retrieve da cookiez. Let 'em cool. (450 + 98.6 = bad)

-5    Participants gather in temple space (or, in true kitchen witch style, use the kitchen area) with the cookies and the Fotamecus Talisman. Form a circle together around the altar (dining table or counter). Cover the altar (table) with an altarcloth (tablecloth) upon which is painted the sigil of Fotamecus. Alternatively, use a piece of butcher paper on which the sigil is scrawled with whatever was handy at the moment. Place cookies upon the altar (table) in a circle around the talisman.

-4    Insert Banishing/Opening Ritual here if so desired (or clean, disinfect, and mop the kitchen).

-3    All participants gather in a circle around altar (table) and join hands, raise them upwards, and look up while calling out loudly, "Fotamecus, We Call Upon You!". Hands are lowered but still held, eyes focus on altar, and all call out, "Fotamecus, Come Witness This!"

-2    Participants break hands, and the HC takes the talisman in his hands and holds it above the altar. All participants place a hand above and below the HCs hands, completely enclosing the talisman. Following the HCs lead, participants begin to breathe deeply in unison, focusing upon the talisman held in the centre of their hands. Participants draw in as much power as they can and force it through their hands into the talisman. Slowly the breathing gets faster and faster. A gnosis should begin creeping up slowly, and as it creeps up, the breathing becomes faster and faster, the group moving together as they breathe power into the talisman.

-1    As gnosis is reached, all participants place their dominant (writing) hand upon their cookie while keeping their other hand on the fist containing the talisman. Then all participants call out, "Fotamecus, Come Feed Us!" and visualise the energy from the talisman running up their arms, into their body, back down the other arm and into the cookies. Continue to call this out throughout this process, not necessarily in unison.

0      When each participant feels they have charged their cookie, they raise their cookie skyward, call out, "Fotamecus, Come Feed Me!" and take a bite of their cookie, their other hand still joined above the altar, still drawing in the power of Fotamecus from the talisman. Feel this power settling in your stomach as you eat the cookie, welling throughout your system, becoming a part of you.

1      After eating the cookie, return the other hand to the centre and wait for all to be done; resume breathing in unison, but slowly and at a comfortable, regular pace. Try to feel the power of Fotamecus spreading throughout your body, the ability to manipulate time at will. Let your mind wander on those thoughts.

2      When all have re-joined hands in the centre, all say in unison, "We Are Fotamecus! Chronos, your time has come!". Then the Head Cook calls out, "Let the Battle be Enjoined!!!" and all give the best battle cry they can.

3      Congratulations, you are now a warrior of Fotamecus! Spend the next few days trying to alter time, possibly with the use of the Fotamecus sigil, possibly without.

4      Either keep the Fotamecus talisman on hand for the next ritual, draw lots to see who gets to keep it, or give it to an individual if there is overwhelming consensus as to who should have it. Or glue a magnet to it and stick it on the refrigerator.

# TIPS:

When impressing the clocks into the cookies, identifying marks can be impressed into the cookie as well to help remember which cookie belongs with which person. Alternatively, each individual cookie can be cooked on aluminium foil that is marked with the participant's name/sigil/identifier.

If there aren't enough clocks to go around, everyone can place their hand on one clock and impress each cookie one at a time together while repeating the phrase for each cookie.

If call-and-repeat must be used for the group lines, it should be called by the HC, and then the HC will repeat it with everyone else in unison.

Any other food that will take an impression of a clock is a suitable substitute for the cookies.

If agreed upon beforehand, instead of simply breathing in unison, all participants can chant the mantric sigil "Fotamecus" in unison with their breathing.

In case anyone missed the obvious symbolism: You're eating a clock (well, a symbol of one at any rate). You are thus conquering it, becoming its master. It's been imbued with the power of Fotamecus and you have drawn that power into yourself, literally digesting it, so that this power becomes a part of you. Duh.

The other key is not to get fixated on the film. We spent plenty of time doing other things where neither film nor video cameras were present.

A set of pathworkings were created for the group. One which takes you on a journey through fast and slow time, a journey towards discovering Fotamecus for yourself. The central image used in the pathworking was that of sitting and watching the cinema screen, watching life unfold, watching and then being in situations in which the subjective experience of time could be moved slowly or faster – at Will, by the power of Fotamecus.

Another pathworking was created to celebrate the festival of Fotamecus – the time when the clocks go forward and back. In these times, when the linear, regular pulse of Chronos clocktime is shown explicitly to be arbitrary and flexible – then all the participants of the Fotamecus film (and indeed those people who have seen the film) would be able to link up and develop our ability to manipulate time. We plan to release these pathworkings alongside the final film.

# Keyman speaks:

January 2001
Fotamecus filmrite: notes on intentions.

At present the focus for developing the intention, the 'intentions' at the heart of the film are;

1) To join the war against linear time, siding with Fotamecus against Chronos, in order to aid liberation from temporal constraints. This is as simple, on some levels, as challenging the norm of a working day constructed around 9-5 time, the bells and whistles of schools and factories ordering our lives. Time is in the first instance a *habit* and the destruction and re-creation of spontaneity and the situation is a battle that has been ongoing on numerous fronts - magical, political, social, artistic and philosophical. This, if you like, is the strategic intention.

2) To aid in a battle or struggle (and I see Chronos as associated with authority and an ordering of lives/life that suppresses life's own nature) you need to find the point of leverage, the tactics of engagement. In this case it is the field of film. To this end I want to create a film that, when watched, echoes and perhaps even establishes a form of rite in itself. To this extent the idea of the film is to make it a 'magical machine', a nomadic experience, caught and moulded, so that the audience finds themselves entangled and enthralled *inside* a magical rite. My only concern here is the 'unintended audience', the audience who might feel duped into participating in something they didn't know was going on. I want to avoid that side of things whilst creating a situation in which the audience leave the theatre/room/TV

45

screen with the sense of having participated in a magical rite. The use of visualisation, both visual and auditory, within the film will aim to implant the primary intention into the psyche of the audience through mantras, sigils and visuals that linger. To a large degree the tactics are nothing other than an extension of what any filmmaker wants to do except that in general this desire to implant something is either artistic/political/social (say something about the world perhaps in order to change it, perhaps in order to merely express oneself) or egotistical (to create a film that is financially successful). The *normal* intentions of a film will be replaced with the magical intention.

3) As an artist-filmmaker I also have a desire to create works of beauty and feel that this aspect of the creation of the beautiful is as much a craft as magic itself. The more successful the film is, as an object of beauty (which does not equate to 'pastoral' or 'idyllic' - scenes, for example, from Angel Heart can be described as beautiful despite their visual horror) the more successful the intention will be.

There will be, before the filming begins, a need to simplify these intentions and achieve a focus for clarity in order to focus the single-pointedness necessary and this single point will be around the final statement of intent surrounding the 'godfigure' Fotamecus. Clarity as to tactics is merely a lever for clarity of final aims.

I hope this clarifies a little. I would say, as a final comment, that there are two aphorisms that inform a lot of my artwork/ filmmaking. The first is by Goddard - 'truth is 24 frames per second'. The second comment is by Picasso who once said that 'when art is properly understood we will be able to paint pictures to cure toothache'. The power of art is in its power not to reflect but to recreate the world - to effect change according to one's will. Art is magical in the true sense. In this sense, then, it is clear that the film is an experiment, a conscious experiment, to effect an open and deliberate union of magic and film, to break the barriers between the two, not so an audience can observe, as passive anthropologists or voracious and vicarious voyeurs, but so that an audience can be themselves transformed and transforming through the operation of the film.

We created three anchor points to aid work with Fotamecus. This would allow people, especially those who had seen the film and thus directly participated in the spawning of the Fotamecus meme, to deploy the power to change time using 'empty-handed magick'. These anchor points are three mudras or hand signs which are derived from one of the deaf sign language systems.

*To slow time down*: still your mind and begin to chant the name Fo-ta-Me-cus over and over until gnosis is attained. Make the slow time mudra. This is done by extending the left arm and pointing it slightly downward. Using the right hand, palm downwards, slowly draw your right hand along your left arm as though stroking it. Let your desire go.

*To make time speed up*: still the mind and chant as before. Make the mudra. Using the thumb, index and forefingers of your right hand. Open these fingers out (with your ring finger and little finger tucked into your palm). Bring your hand back so that your hand, three fingers extended is by the side of your head, on the same level as your eye. Tense your arm and then, when you are ready, fling your arm forward so that your right hand is fully extended and bring your fingers together as though catching an insect. Let your desire go.

*To 'reset' the space-time continuum:* Again, still your mind and chant the name Fotamecus.
When ready place both hands on your forehead, with thumbs pointing upward. Pull your hands away from your head as though you are pulling something back (eg a curtain) and bring your thumbs into the palms of each hand. Mentally or aloud thank Fotamecus.

As Fotamecus is a new god it really likes to come out and play, so don't worry about struggling to reach plus four states of gnosis before you deploy the mudra. A light state of trance and the characteristic 'disinterested interest' that often works well for empty-handed magick is fine.

These mudras formed part of the main Fotamecus working. This was conducted at a place called Black Cap on the Sussex South Downs not far from Brighton. The evening of the filming saw us carrying vast amounts of gear (with the help of a number of runners) up a long track and into some woodland that we had already identified as the site for the ritual. Keyman had been observing the place for a while, a dense grove of beech and sycamore, fairly isolated and with a welcoming atmosphere.

The preparation for the ritual included entertaining visits from the local constabulary, National Trust warden, local farmers and gamekeeper. Considering that we had already applied for and been granted permission to be there it seemed as though the forces of awe and boredom had a little too much time on their hands. Finally the scene was set. Huge banners bearing sigils that we had created as part of the preparatory work were hung from the trees, lights flooded the grove and we donned our ceremonial robes and masks.

The sound of the generator. The deep shadows cast by the lighting rig. The wind in the trees…
We begin by holding hands, taking a moment to be silent before we begin. Brother rhino, Brother Kondwani and I blessed the camera, as a member of our group, as the transmitter of our word, as the creator of images and the recorder of our work.

Fotamecus! Your time has come!

The aim was to give birth to Fotamecus through the film. Our plan to concentrate the Fotamecus egregore into the one thing that it could not tolerate – a clock. Our intention is to create a focus and a road which will attract the Fotamecus egregore and funnel its power into the timepiece. Then, as the clock is destroyed, so the light (that great definer of time) from the burning clock will enter the camera, expose the film and thus the energy of the ritual will be literally captured on the stock. The clocks hands would be set at 10:07 – check out a clock shop next time you pass one and see how many clocks are set at seven minutes past ten. Why? Well it makes the clock look happy, like a smiling face. Happy time.

Morrigan symbolically cleared the working site using a broomstick, and I walked the edge of the circle, calling for the protection of the spirits of the place. Sister A-Image lit the candle in the east and using incense invoked the spirits of Air. South and Fire was summoned by Brother rhino. throwing salt through the red candle flame to bring the power of fire into the earth with us. Sister Tao poured water and lit the Western candle, summoning the spirits of water. Brother Kondwani. held up a clod of earth and, lighting the candle in the North summoned the spirits there.

Fotamecus your time has come, Fotamecus we call on you!

We each began the Fotamecus mantra, slowly, gently letting the sound wash over us. And as we did so Sister Tao created the egg that would be the womb of the spirit. Drawing with flour on the floor the sacred space is formed. As she did this Brother rhino created a spiral. Again marked in flour, from the tip of the egg, round into the centre of the circle. This would be the road for the spirit.

When this was done the chanting stopped and we cast the Fotamecus slow time mudra.

All cry 'Fotamecus your time has come, Fotamecus we call on you!'

Those on the edge of the egg begin the Fotamecus mantra, rapidly and with varying tempo and volume.

Lamps are placed to show the spirit the way along the spiral path by Brother Kondwani. The flames from the lamps are like the landing lights of an astral airstrip. Together Brother Kondwani and Sister A-Image kindle the central fire. The pyramid of sticks in the centre of the circle blazes up, its orange glow transgresses the hard shadows of the limelights. Smoke rises into the grove and is captured by the wind.

Again the chanting ceases and we all make the fast time mudra.

All cry 'Fotamecus your time has come, Fotamecus we call on you'.

Those on the edge of the egg begin the Fotamecus mantra - freestyle!

Morrigan picks up the clock and walks the spiral path to the centre of the egg.
I follow with a brush, pot of red paint and weapons of destruction (a sword and club). We are following the spiral path, into the Orphic egg, following the lamps that light the spirit road, towards the heart of the sacred space. We are drawing Fotamecus into the space, into the concentrated zone of power…

The sigil of Fotamecus is painted on the clock by Morrigan, it is then set down beside the fire. The paint gleams wet like blood.

Both Morrigan and I begin to shake using Sedir, seething movements to get into trance. We are overbreathing, forcing our bodies to become drunk on oxygen. Around us the Fotamecus mantra builds and we feel the spirit entering the space much faster than would normally be expected. Fotamecus is obviously eager to be born!

We shake, building the energy and then the moment has come. I provide Morrigan with the Sword and I take up the club, she swings and brings the blade down on the clock, I follow with the club and the talisman is destroyed. The Fotamecus mantra rolls around the grove; we pick up the remains of the clock and hurl them into the flames.

And banish with laughter!

Later that night we eat and drink, deciding to stay in the woods. For some inexplicable reason we have all forgotten to bring sleeping bags and so spend the night huddled in the Fotamecus sigil banners. The fire burns down, the generator is silenced. Owls hoot in the darkness.

So where is the camera in all this? Two video and one film camera are trained on the ritual. The film camera has been allowed the right to call 'stop' and halt our rite at any moment. But this didn't happen, nor, it later transpires, did any of the cameras actually get a shot of the clock being destroyed. There is a strange sense in the air, not of unease, but of something unfinished. Of course the film will not be completed for some months to come but it's something else. As though the ritual isn't really over…

We mused about the idea of using explosives and filming a clock exploding, trying to capture that elusive moment that the camera missed on the night. Retrospectively, retroactively sealing the spell. Whatever we were to do next, what we really needed was another clock to destroy.

It was a week or two later, while thinking about the fact that we needed to complete the ritual, to finish the 'capture' of the spirit onto celluloid, I found another clock. As I walked down to the train station (the location that features at the beginning of the Fotamecus film) I found it, a big clock, the kind they have in offices. There it was, on the pavement, a dead ringer for the timepiece that we had dispatched in the woodland, and what time did it say? Seven minutes past ten!

Months later we returned to Black Cap for the final filming of the ritual elements of the movie. In the cold November mist we hoisted the Fotamecus sigil banners into the air and donned our robes once more. This section was simple, filming us going to the top of the hill. In that classic way of movies the start was being filmed after the end.

Slowly we ascended the hill, with Keyman calling us onward as each shot was taken. Brother rhino wore the clock around his neck, changing the time at each cut. (His chronometric lamen led him to be temporarily possessed by the spirit of Flava Flav.)

Finally we were back in the woods and we held hands once more. There was a moment of silence and Keyman spoke, thanking the spirit of the place, the spirit of Fotamecus and drawing the ritual to a close. And as we stood in that wood, far away from the world of clocking on and off we felt the ritual come to an end.

But for Fotamecus the fun was only just beginning.

# Mahakali Maya

It's odd the things one learns. 'Kali Temples have a nasty habit of catching fire' - that's one that I now know to be a fact. The friend who sent me that advisory email quoted examples of two temples, build by various friends, dedicated to the bloody goddess of time and death. The first was a bender structure that had gone up in smoke, the second a tent that, during one particularly dramatic ritual, had been entirely destroyed by a conflagration.

In accordance with this the wise wizard always packs a trusty fire extinguisher!

The space for the rituals was fabulous. Brother rhino. had helped take a squat on Viaduct Road, the building had been workshop premises, built in that apparently timeless mid-twentieth-century-brick-but-featureless style. The narrow staircase led down to the bottom two floors which we were going to use. The only permanent inhabitant of the squat - Snoop, seemed unconcerned about our antics in a kind of off-hand sort of a way.

The rooms themselves were behind boarded up shop fronts, bone shatteringly cold concrete floors and featuring a strangely institutional looking sink in the corner. Here we would create a potent temporal autonomous zone. Here we could build and install our own art, our own creations. Brother rhino and Sister mill mill led the project, they focused the form of the space and, aided and abetted by myself, Brother Kondwani, Sister Artemis, and a loose network of others, this outlaw chamber was transformed into a place of power and of magick.

The chamber walls were covered with white drapes from floor to ceiling. On the floor was painted the muladhara lotus. The base chakra, that place from which all our basic drives spring – the drive to feed, to flee, to fight and form territory. This is the material realm. The red four-petaled lotus, some three meters wide. The flower sat upon a mountain of skulls. Photocopied grinning white bone faces, thousands of them painstakingly stuck to the floor and varnished. Thus the lotus sits upon the charnel ground of the earth, just as our lives build upon and are supported by the bones of our dead ancestors…

Brother rhino strikes the singing bowl and begins…

The beginning of the ritual is for us to be consciousness of the reality and meaning of this installation. Sri Parameshvari puja is our first working.

Now we come to the Muladhara Lotus. Deep at the base of your spine. Placed below your genitals and above your anus: Its head hangs downwards. It has four petals of deep crimson, on which shine the letters Va, Sh, S, & Sa, of brilliant gold. Root support of the sound mandala universe.

Here is the bottom of creation!

The Dominant Para- Sri Parameshvari!
Listen, whilst you have this rare chance of liberty and opportunity!
Here, we die before death and become the twice born!
These are your four aims!

Dharma-Right thinking
Artha- Acquisition of wealth
Kama- Sexuality
Moksha-Liberation

Conquering four Asuras respectively:
Ignorance.
Revulsion.
Attachment.
Delusion.

May Sri MahaMaya Kali Kalaratrisvarupini extinguish what is left!

Here! Listen! In this endless cycle of Death and Rebirth, which is entirely without gates; is the four-fold Dhara-Mandala, shining yellow, Tattva of Earth Beautiful like lightning.

A blue circle rests upon the lotus, without gates because in this place, the world, all things are linked to the cycle of birth, sex, death and rebirth.

> Cohesive principle of solidity.
> Matter is at its densest here,
> This is the seat of the fat one, being all categories that exist.
> Here we are nourished by the smell of food, the release of sleep,
> we wash, we clean, we fuck, and we fight. Here, resistance is
> at its highest.

> This is the part of your myth you can touch! Here nobly born!
> Not anywhere else! Here where our everyday lives are situated,
> where your beauty unfolds from sleep everyday!

We sit not being asked to imagine these things for here it is! In actuality, we are seated upon the lotus, in the World of the world. Our circle (there are some ten participants) sits upon the earth as on a raft.

Brother rhino leads us through the mantras and meaning of this space. His movements are wild and intoxicated like the sadus I've seen raving in Tamil Nadu. We are isolated from the world, cut off from the everyday and yet we are profoundly aware of the reality of all this, the cold of the concrete floor, the sounds from the road outside. This is hyperreality.

> Nuclear seed bija of this Tattva is LAM – of the nature of
> diamonds.
> Within the bindu of the mantra, seated in abundant opulence on
> a gigantic red lotus, in pure bliss, Mighty Maha Ganesha
> chuckles and eats sweets. Filling all dimensions with his
> incomprehensible bulk. He is the Seer-poet of the crossroads.
> Beloved boy of beginnings. Lord of the Gana Spirit horde.
> Namah! Namah!

> Oh Destroyer, you are so fat and we love you so much!

> You are the body of material pleasure,
> You are the sense lord,
> You are the feeder,

The food & the fed.

AUM GAM.

Hear us oh pork chop champion of the oppressed, you carry in your arms the Child Creator Brahma, Glowing rainbow hued Supercontext.
The perfect lover who's MahaMantra-

HARE KRSNA HARE KRSNA
KRSNA KRSNA HARE HARE
HARE RAMA HARE RAMA
RAMA RAMA HARE HARE

Is resplendent like the young sun dispelling the sheer terror of the aroused Kundalini.
Lord of desire, the self-born supreme divinity of lust, impeller of creation.
Proud adolescent, riding a parrot, bow of sugarcane, the bowstring a line of bees, your five arrows of heavenly fragrance incite wild passion for the joy of union, in fields, by a lake, in cities, towns and villages, love is the pivot on which we turn! Jai!

Brother rhino's hands sweep across the mandala on the floor, indicating the elements of the yantra, building the space-text of the puja with movements and words.

Here near the mouth of the Nadi called Vajra, in the pericarp there constantly shines the beautifully luminous and soft lightning triangle Tripura. There is always and everywhere the seat of Shakti. The Yoni, of the nature of the three worlds, the three times, the three gunas; Sattva, Rajas & Tamas.

Here in Tamas. Inertia. Decay. Where all forms return is Sakti Dakini Kali Kalaratrisvarupini. Burning like 10 million suns. Seated on an unfolding red lotus, smashing the pride of this degenerate age, the presided of the yuga of blood, corruption and hypocrisy.

Her name is the last breath, she who strikes terror into the hearts of the uninitiated; uncontrollable, holding in her right hands the spear and lotus, and in her left the sword and skull cup filled with wine. She is fierce in temper and shows her teeth. Addicted to the spilling of blood. Primary Adya Shakti you crush the whole host of enemies. You are plump of body and fond of rice pudding. As all colours disappear into black, so all beings return into you. Darkness within Darkness the gateway to all understanding.

Inside is Svayambu in his Linga form, beautiful like precious gems, he is revealed by Knowledge and Meditation, and is of the nature of a fresh new leaf. As the cool rays of lighting and the full moon charm desire, so does his beauty. Diamond point of consciousness. The Deva who resides here happily is in created forms like an irresistible whirlpool. You are mighty Shushumna Self-contained reality manifestation vajra technology of the nature of our own central nervous system. Inert, like a corpse. The senses are dead. All you perceive is dreaming Kundalini. MahaMaya, fine as a lotus stalk, she is the world-bewilderer, gently covering the mouth of Supercontext comprehension with her own.

Now you perceive the Gayatri of the Kali-Yuga. Listen and be liberated.

The twilight language washes over us. Some of our company know these symbols and can plainly see the linga in the lotus. For others this evocative text is suggestive, exotic, a relentless barrage of images, a rich word feast with the occasional jarring description to prevent complacency. For all the truth is overwhelming. Here we are in the world, on the lotus. The text of the puja is only a pretty statement of the strangeness of the real world. The effect is like those first few moments when you are waiting for the acid to kick in. You know that somehow you will soon be tripping and that you can watch, expectantly, for the very first inkling of the drug effect. The psychedelic state always sneaks up on one; from the corner of your eye, from the edges of awareness and from an unexpected direction - like the universe saying 'boo!' and catching itself sleeping...

The temple is dedicated to Kali – this is her place. She is the goddess in the muladhara chakra, she liberates us when death comes. She teaches the tantras and creates the world of form, she is time.

The squat contains her symbols. Upstairs there is a small devotional shrine that each of us knelt at on our entry to the building. On it the yantra of the goddess, her triangles and four gates. Red candles and incense, a bowl of water and red flowers are her offerings.

Now in the temple all eyes are firmly fixed on her altar.

Red and green silks hang from the ceiling. They frame an image of Kali as the beautiful and terrible Mother, in one hand she holds a skull dripping blood, and in another an AK47 assault rifle. Round her head are love hearts in a rainbow of colours. Around her are other forms, Mahakali standing upon Shiva, her ten arms raised with weapons of war and liberation. Below her the sandalwood sculpture of Ganesha fat and gorgeous. Offerings are clustered around the big bellied elephant headed god; perfume, water, flowers, fruit. More images of Kali fill the altar; the goddess as an aged woman, the goddess as P.J.Harvey wearing her T-shirt urging 'lick my legs'.

On the floor, beneath the altar space resting on the mountain of skulls, is the fetish.

The fetish has been made from newspapers with sigils scrawled upon them, crushed into balls and stuck into a vague pyramidal shape using a quick drying builder's foam. Over this red wax has been poured, creating a structure that resembles a bloody hunk of meat. Hair and nail clippings of the assembled company have also been incorporated. Into this, red candles have been stuck and upon and around it we have decorated the altar to befit the goddess.

There is a huge spear, a multitude of skulls and bones. Wine and fruit, sweets, incense and red flowers in great abundance.

Jai Mahakali! Praise Kali!

Like the twilight language of the puja the altar is at once simple and overwhelmingly opulent. It is baroque and gothic, cultures and ideas clash within its form. Signs of care and love and safety and images of war or violence and of sudden death.

Svayambu tames the multiplicity of Her form, which coils like the Conch shell KRSNA blew on the battlefield of the ancestors.

Her of the soft golden limbs, primal ratio, Self-Sentient reality patterning, here in forms concealed, having every single characteristic, hand removing fear.

Her neurosomatic response is that of a strong flash of young strong lightning. Her sweet biological murmur is like the hum of swarms of cellular algorithms resonating implicitly. Melodious nuclear seed syllable poetry of perceptual machinery – like immense clouds of love-mad bees.

Here reigns the dominant Parameshvari.
We do this Puja as a dedication to Sri Parameshvari. The awakened of eternal knowledge. She is the Omnipotent Kala who is wonderfully skilful to create, and is subtler than the subtlest. She is the receptacle of that continuous stream of ambrosia which flows from the eternal bliss. By Her radiance it is that the universe and this cauldron is illumined. She is the Devi Dakini by name, Her four arms shine with beauty, and her eyes are brilliant red. She is like the lustre of a million suns rising at once and the same time. She is the carrier of the revelation of the ever-pure intelligence.
It is she who maintains all the beings of the world, by means of inspiration and exploration, poetry, verse, in sequence or otherwise. She shines in the cavity of the red lotus like a chain of brilliant handmade children's lanterns.
She who is of the nature of light and sound, shining in the forehead like the lustrous rainbow of Brahma. In the crown of the head united like the luminous white shine of the moon, and

in the heart like the never-setting splendourous sun. May She, by the means of the three mighty syllables -

KRIM
HRIM
SRIM

Speedily destroy all our impurities.

(Pause)

Macrobindu
Repository of all manifestation in complexity and variety. Basis of all vibration, movement, form.
Starting point in the unfolding of space/time as well as the last point of its ultimate integration. Extensionless mathematical point of pervading consciousness. Zero dimensions.

AUM
(Pause)

The eight–fold yoga
The six regions of the body
The five states
They have left and gone
Totally erased
And in the open
Void
We are left
Amazed
There is but a red-rounded moon
A fountain of white milk
For delight
The Unobtainable bliss
Has engulfed us
A precipice
Of light

Get Up
Wake Up
Be Strong

I Formally close this Puja

Brother rhino strikes the singing bowl and we listen to the sound dwindle, merging at last with the background vibration of the world. We are back, changed and yet nothing has changed. The mantra and the worship has served to place us directly in the muladhara. We know what we must do, the injunction is as clear as the four aims:

Right thinking
Acquisition of wealth
Sexuality
Liberation

Though the first puja has closed we are still here, still seated in the muladhara chakra, sitting on the hard floor on the red lotus atop a mountain of skulls.

Through this puja the working space is opened, the sequence of what was to become four rituals in honour of Kali is begun.

But before we move more deeply into the body of the dark goddess, Brother rhino opens the space with an invocation to that other ruler of the base chakra. The elephant Lord Ganesh. Since this ritual is at the beginning of a sequence of work, and the installation of this space, we petition the blessing of the god who opens the way. Ganesha is Brother rhino's special protector and friend. He is god of riches, of wealth, of sweets and joy. The sandalwood image of Ganesha sits, fat and resplendent on the altar, and winks.

We break for a short time and share water, tobacco and cannabis then Brother rhino once more strikes the singing bowl and cries:

OM GAM

# Dhyana:

Residing at the true centre of the perceptual universe, within the immense island continent Mountain Meru, Simultaneously illumined by the distant light of the setting moon and warmed by the early light of the rising sun; cooled by the four fragrant winds of heaven. Inside a perfumed garden of sandalwood sweetness, enmeshed in fine, leafy creepers, lapped by the honey-sweet waters of paradise.

In the distance vibrates the soft echo of eternal drums. There beneath verdant, immortal trees resonates the primordial muladhara lotus, and within, is mighty MahaGanapati!

Great bellied, his awesome bulk fills all directions. One tusk and ten arms, dispelling fear and granting boons!

A tawny and resplendent dumpy conqueror!
Winner of hearts and master of poets, infinite and consciousness personified, the destroyer of obstacles! Huge and gigantic, immediately present beyond all points in time!

Omkara Ganesha!

Around us, at the eight points in space we imagine each Ganesha form, raising up in glorious colour and vibrant power. Creating an eight-rayed star of unbendable Gana power!

Brother rhino points at each place of manifestation as he names the form that rises from the lotus beneath us.

In the East! In realms of red gana spirit hordes, the hideously deformed Vikata Ganesha conquers the lust demon Kamasura!

In the South-East! Following the rising sun into realms of purple, corpulent belly Lambodara Ganesha utterly devours the anger demon Krodasura, liberating worlds!

In the South! Elephant face Gajanana transforms the greed of Lobhasura into realms of yellow Ganas at his command!

In the South-West! Big belly Mahodra Ganesha vanquishes the demon of delusion Mohasura in fields of blue Gana laughter!

In the West! Kshipra Ganesha, He who is easy to appease, smothers the demon of intoxication, Matasura in the midst of green Gana armies!

In the North-West! The silver Gana horde of jealousy ruled by Matsara is dominated completely! Vakratunda, the Deva wielding the unquestionable power of the twisting trunk laughs on!

In the North! Smoky Dhumravana smites gold Abhimasura into formless void, ending his attachment to causality from beyond time!

In the final direction! North-East of Mountain Meru! Incredible Vighnaraja Ganesha consumes Istasura, in orange realms of demonic tendencies, thus removing and transforming all fear into abodes of bliss!

OM MAHAGANAPATI NAMAH!

OM GAM!

The energy rises. From the hyperreal fact of the first ritual the delight begins to surface. The muladhara chakra is the realm of death, of obligation and of desire, but sometimes desire can be fun! Attachment is only sorrow if you want it to be. As Brother rhino gets more enraptured so the excitement, the joy of worshipping Ganesha, such a jolly and powerful god, takes hold! We begin to be transported. Some people have eyes open but rolled up into their heads, for others hands are clapped in prayer. And this praying isn't the contrition of confession but the praise of elation, rapture. For others their bodies rock back and forth like Jews in the synagogue. We dwell in devotion, praising the god who likes sugar plums!

By meditating thus; Pure of disposition by deep and musical words, We serve the foremost of the Devas, and seek immediate dissolution of my sins, to gain all virtues, to seek blessings of Lord MahaGanapati through this form, and through his blessing attain wisdom.

Be pleased to come here, O Gajanana, You who are dear to Shiva, You who are dear to Parvarti, the refuge of those without refuge, all-knowing!

We exalt you Lord Siddhi Vinayaka through this Beautiful form!

Feel your belly to be a void within you. As you breathe, see this void beginning to fill with a scarlet mist. Gradually, the mist begins to form a shape - the shape of the Elephant-headed one, Ganesha.

Ganesha, vermilion-coloured, with the head of an elephant and the body of a man, whose vehicle is a mouse.

Big of belly, with ears like winnowing baskets, he holds a pomegranate in his trunk, and the crescent moon is upon his forehead. In his four hands he holds a tusk, an elephant goad, a noose, and gives the gesture of granting boons.

The tusk he holds represents service

The goad prods us along our path

The noose reminds us of that which binds us

To his favoured he grants all boons

His ears, like winnowing baskets, sift truth from non-truth

His twisting trunk shows us the power of strength and discrimination

His vehicle, the Mouse, is for cunning, and subtlety.

Meditate upon the qualities of the Ganesha within you - he has the strength and wisdom of an elephant; the intelligence of man; the cunning and subtlety of a mouse. He is the Lord of the Ganas, the demon-horde of Shiva. He is the bringer of luck, the remover of obstacles. Son of Shiva and Parvati, beloved of gods and men alike.

At this point each of us breaths the power of our internal Ganesha into the sandalwood carving of the god. We breathe our power into him so that, like a lamp, he can radiate his power back to the whole group. Thus rather than the more usual process of creating a focus of power and then absorbing it we each share our power, transmitted by the image as the focus.

Ganesha is like that, there does not need to be any selfish hoarding up of siddhi. What is the point of hoarding the energy of the god who breaks down barriers? Ganesha is Jupiter, the all-giver, the bountiful prince who, generous of heart, blesses with boons all who seek his aid.

Once the image has been filled by the power of our externalised Ganesha it is ready for worship. It is no longer a mere block of wood but a vessel for our own power which itself is a tributary from the great river of Ganesha in universal reality. Brother rhino makes offerings to the vivified image.

> Gam, Obeisance to Ganapati (pour water from first bowl into other two)
> Gam this water. Gam Gam Gam Hum Hum Om Gam Ganapati Namah
> [Offer first bowl to Ganesha] - Gam, this is for sipping
> [Offer second bowl to Ganesha] - Gam, this is for bathing
> [Dab perfume on head of Ganesha] - Gam, this is perfume
> [Cense Image around Ganesha] - Gam, this is incense, this is for prayer
> [Offer Candle to Ganesha] - Gam, this is flame, this is for sacrifice [Offer Food to Ganesha] - Gam, this is food, this is for sustenance
> [Offer Flower to Ganesha] - Gam, this is flower, this is for experience
> [Make music to Ganesha] - Gam, this is music, this is for enjoyment
> Take these offerings O Sri Mahaganapati, bestow siddhi upon us!

At this stage of the puja Brother rhino takes up his prayer beads. This call and response sequence some of us have done before and it is always a powerful and funny event. The 108 titles and attributes of Ganesha are called and the participants respond, repeating the words with hearts full of gladness.

Salutations to him who is our refuge
Salutations to the one with the wondrous form
Salutations to the foremost presider
Salutations to him who is the fire within
Salutations to the first-born
Salutations to the unborn one
Salutations to him who is without impurity
Salutations to him who is worshipped by all
Salutations to the manifestation of the unmanifest
Salutations to the inexhaustible one
Salutations to the inexhaustible one
Salutations to the granter of devotees' desires
Salutations to the destroyer of devotees' obstacles
Salutations to the one who loves pomegranates
Salutations to him who is celibate
Salutations to him who is free from aversion to the Divine
Salutations to the foremost knower of Brahman
Salutations to him to whom intelligence is dear
Salutations to him who is powerful
Salutations to him who wields the discus
Salutations to the wearer of the moon on his head
Salutations to the ingenious one
Salutations to the one with four arms
Salutations to the skilful one
Salutations to the self-controlled one
Salutations to the compassionate one
Salutations to the resplendent one
Salutations to the courageous one
Salutations to him who is fond of durva and bilva
Salutations to him who has two mothers
Salutations to him who is fond of the twice born
Salutations to the one with a single tusk
Salutations to the lord of the multitudes
Salutations to him who has an elephant's face
Salutations to him who wields the mace

Salutations to the son of Gauri
Salutations to the lord of planets
Salutations to him who transcends all qualities
Salutations to him who is lion-like
Salutations to the rapturous one
Salutations to him who holds the sugarcane bow
Salutations to the bestower of Indra's power
Salutations to the one with matted locks
Salutations to the embodiment of wisdom
Salutations to him who works incessantly
Salutations to the bestower of absolute happiness
Salutations to the destroyer of Kali's impurity
Salutations to the embodiment of time
Salutations to him who is love
Salutations to the beloved one
Salutations to him who upholds the mountains
Salutations to the one with the big belly
Salutations to the source of all illusory power
Salutations to him who is praised by sages
Salutations to him whose vehicle is the mouse
Salutations to he who wears a cobra as a sacred thread
Salutations to him who is without blemish
Salutations to the destroyer of wickedness
Salutations to him for whom there is no other
Salutations to the wielder of the noose and goad
Salutations to him who is feared by ambitious men
Salutations to the blissful one
Salutations to the pure one
Salutations to the God worshipped by Rama
Salutations to the creator
Salutations to him whose form is existence, knowledge, bliss
Salutations to him who is fond of playing with his mother
Parvati, daughter of the mountain lord
Salutations to the powerful one
Salutations to him who is fond of the Sama Veda
Salutations to the attentive one
Salutations to the supporter of the worlds
Salutations to the dearest son of Shiva's spouse

Salutations to the bestower of all perfections
Salutations to the bestower of all fulfilment
Salutations to the son of Shiva
Salutations to the omnipresent Self
Salutations to the peaceful one
Salutations to the peaceful one
Salutations to the unchanging one
Salutations to him whose lotus feet sages worship
Salutations to the bestower of fulfilment
Salutations to the auspicious one
Salutations to the first-born, Skanda's brother
Salutations to him whose eyes are the sun and moon
Salutations to the bestower of prosperity
Salutations to him with the beautiful throat
Salutations to him who manifests prosperity
Salutations to the lord of Lakshmi
Salutations to him who has a stout neck
Salutations to he who is pleased with praise
Salutations to the pure one
Salutations to him with ears like winnowing fans
Salutations to him who is a vast ocean of sweetness more
charming than the god of love
Salutations to him who acts independently
Salutations to the self-established one
Salutations to the content one
Salutations to him who holds the blue lotus
Salutations to the lord of speech
Salutations to the bestower of boons
Salutations to the bestower of speech
Salutations to the lord of the wise
Salutations to the controller of destiny
Salutations to the lord of obstacles
Salutations to the remover of obstacles
Salutations to him who is free from fear

For some of the salutations memory fails and the company are sent laughing and smiling into a mumble, for others the message is so clear that we sing out strong. As the salutations progress so the image on the altar seems to smile.

The prayers continue – we are quieter and deeper in trance, deeper in the devotional space. The chattering laughter and fun of the salutations gives way to a deeper ecstasy, a warm happy feeling punctuated by the occasional grin and cries of 'Jai' - 'Praise'.

OM LAM
We bow to Ganesha
You are clearly the Tattva.
You alone are the Creator. You alone are the Maintainer.
You alone are the Destroyer.
Of all this you are certainly Brahma.
You plainly are the essence.
Always I speak Amrita. The Truth I speak.

Protect me. Protect the speakers. Protect the hearers. Protect the givers. Protect the holders. Protect the disciple that repeats. Protect that in the East. Protect that in the South. Protect that in the West. Protect that in the North. Protect that above. Protect that below. Everywhere protect. Protect me everywhere!

You are Speech. You are Consciousness. You are Bliss. You are Brahma. You are Being-Consciousness-Bliss. You are the Non-Dual. You are plainly Brahma. You are Knowledge. You are Intelligence.

You create this world. You maintain this world. This entire world is seen in you. You are Earth, Water, Fire, Air, Aethyr. You are beyond the four measures of speech. You are beyond the Three Gunas. You are beyond the three bodies. You are beyond the three times. You are always situated in the Muladhara. You are the being of the three Shaktis. You are always meditated upon by Yogins. You are Brahma, you are Vishnu, you are Rudra, You are Agni, You are Vayu, You are the Moon, You are the Sun, you are Brahma, Bhur-Bhuvah-Svar.

'Ga' the first syllable, after that the first letter, beyond that 'm', then the half-moon all together. Joined with "Om" this is the mantra-form.

Letter 'Ga' the first form, letter 'a' the middle form, 'm' the last form. Bindu the higher form, Nada the joining together, Samhita the junction. This is the Vidya of Lord Ganesha. Ganaka is the seer, Nricad-Gayatri the metre, Sri Mahaganapati the God. "Om Ganapataye Namah."

Let us think of the one-toothed, let us meditate on the crooked trunk, may that tusk direct us.

One tusk, four arms, carrying noose and goad, with His hands dispelling fear and granting boons, with a mouse as his banner. Red, with a big belly, with ears like winnowing baskets, wearing red, with limbs smeared in red scent, truly worshipped with red flowers.

To the devoted a merciful Deva, the Maker of the World, the Prime Cause, who at the beginning of creation was greater than gods and men.

He who always meditates thus is a Yogin above Yogins.

Hail to the Lord of Vows, hail to Ganapati, hail to the First Lord, hail unto you, to the Big-Bellied, One-tusked, Obstacle-destroyer, the Son of Shiva, to the Boon-Giver, Hail, hail.

Any who study this Atharva Shira moves towards Brahma. They are always blissful. Any obstacles do not bind them. They are liberated from the five greater and the five lesser sins. Evening meditation destroys the unmeritorious actions of the night. At both evening and morning they are liberated from the bad and attain Dharma, Artha, Kama and Moksha.

Any who wants something may accomplish it by 1000 recitations of this. Any who sprinkle Ganapati with this become eloquent. Any who recites this on a fourth day becomes a knower of Vidya. An Artharva saying, "They who move towards Brahma Vidya are never afraid". Anyone who worships with fried grains becomes famous and becomes intelligent. Worship with sweet-meat (modaka) gains the desired fruit. Worshipping with samit and ghee all is attained, all is gained. Anyone who makes eight Brahmans understand this becomes like the sun's rays. In a solar eclipse, in a great river, or in front of an image having recited this they get accomplished in the mantra, and become liberated from great obstacles. They are freed from great misfortunes.

Salutations to you again and again!
Salutations to you who are the universe!

We formally close this puja.

Brother rhino strikes the singing bowl again and smiles contentedly.[10]

## The Second Puja

Once again we meet on the lotus flower of the muladhara chakra. This time we praise Krishna as the lord of sated desire, the fulfilment of the promise of existence. This is our Krisha, not as the ascetic, celibate lord. We praise Krishna as the possibility of desire being met through the infinite power of Maya. We praise Krisha as the lover of the Gopi girls.

Then for the goddess, to Mahakali we make our dedication. We press our fingerprints in red ink onto her yantra which hangs in the temple. This sigil is left in the space to show our commitment to the work.

This second ceremony is calm, not sedate but gentle and we are impressed by the ease with which we are being admitted to the realm of Mahakali. I comment as much to a Sister as we walk our way homeward.

This is the calm before the storm.

## The Third Puja

Even before we begin there is a power in the room.

As for the previous two rituals we prepare the space using the Gnostic Pentagram ritual. The first visualisation is of the goddess Tara, amazingly attractive sixteen year old shakti with firm breasts and radiant with power. She is installed within each of us by imagination and within her a rotating character of the seed mantra that is her name. Her generous power floods out from us and connects all beings.

The imagery is strong and clear – something is here, here in the temple. There is a power here, I can feel it...

The second phase of this puja is an invocation of Mahakali in her darkest forms, the goddess of guilt, of old age, of knotted anger and despair. In her we destroy all restrictions that we have, we ask for the tongues of our enemies to be silenced, that they should be nailed to the earth. We ask to come through and to learn from the frustration, the disfigurement she represents. We summon the form of Kali to come after her, the lady of the tantras, goddess of black magick.

Then at the nadir of this working, in the darkest, most destructive part of the Kali cycle, we take sigils that we have each prepared, set them on fire and cast them into the pot that was first used to create the wax fetish (that crouches in a gloriously obscene fashion beneath the altar).

At first the flames begin to lick the inside of the pot and we can hear the hissing of the remaining wax as it begins to catch, each sigil acting like a wick, encouraging the temperature to go up and up. For the first time in the whole sequence of rituals the temple is warm as a glorious spout of yellow fire heats the room.

Finally somebody suggests that the flame, which by now is some four-foot high, looks a bit dodgy and we should do something.

We start to get nervous and finally Brother rhino reaches for the fire extinguisher and sprays the flames with a single burst. It's a powder extinguisher and as the white dust passes into the vessel nothing seems to happen. So, encouraged by the fact that everybody else is making for the door, Brother rhino lets rip, the fiery cauldron skids across to the floor towards Sister Artemis and me!

Finally the flames are out. Keyman rips open the back door (jokingly referred to as the emergency exit at previous meetings). It is impossible to see across the room as the extinguisher powder floats around. Suddenly we realise that we can't breath – some people vanish upstairs and some of us finally get out the back door. On the other side of the door is somebody else's garden as the building backs directly onto their property. For a moment we are concerned that somebody will emerge from the house opposite ('don't worry we're just having a spot of Kali trauma!').

But more significantly Snoop, the only full-time resident of the squat, comes rushing downstairs, past some members of the temple who have elected to try to get to air by going upstairs. He is cross, 'What the fuck! You've set my fucking house on fire…'

Brother rhino eventually disappears upstairs with Snoop and slowly, as the dust clears, people come back downstairs to the temple. We are wafting the air using the drapes by the door, trying to and get some fresh air into the room.

Upstairs we can hear the fight breaking out, shouting and screaming but no obvious noises of violence. My gut twists with that horrid and yet somehow pleasurably intense sensation of adrenaline. But none of us need to go and break it up. Brother rhino returns downstairs and tells us, 'just in case you didn't know, me and Snoop have just had a fight'.

Brother Kondwani suggests that we banish the space and Sister mill mill suggests that we should decamp to her place just to finish the puja.

Every surface in the room is covered with a fine white dust, a dust like charnel ash. The substance sacred to Kali is ash, the only thing that is left when the fire of desire has burnt us all up. Sacred ash the only remains of raised kundalini.

We determinedly go through the Gnostic Pentagram ritual and forcibly earth the energy. We then leave the building which is still filled with a tangible anger.

Back in Sister mill mill's house we crowd into her living room, light candles and enjoy the steady warmth of her gas fire. On her mantelpiece are images of Ganesha, Kali, and the ladybird, which is her power animal. Brother rhino takes us through the last of the puja. It is like coming home to harbour after being out on a wide stormy sea. We are safe.[11]

## The Fourth Puja

The temple has been cleaned up and looks immaculate. Fresh flowers and fruit decorate the space. Brother rhino has negotiated with Snoop that we can hold one last ritual.

Once more we sit on the muladhara lotus, upon a mound of grinning skulls. Now we have come through the lunar month together, we the twice born, we Kings and Queens have been reborn through Kali, through the dark goddess.

We burn the yantra that was our dedication, this time the flames rise and die without incident. We begin to remove those precious things from the altar, certain skulls, paintings, power objects.

The temple is closed. For many of us the effect of these rituals is that old ties are cut. For Brother rhino his friendship with Snoop was over, for Sister Eris the schism in her previous magickal group finally split asunder. For Sister Artemis and me, we would finally put an end to some relationships that had been dragging us down for literally years. None of these things was easy, the Kali pujas certainly brought things to a head and sometimes it is certainly 'better out that in'.

Yet for the group who met in that squat, who sat together on the red lotus, this working helped to forge a new alliance of magicians. Fire can destroy and it can forge. I have seen it with my own eyes.

You are sitting on the red lotus right now.

# Halloween $33^1/_3$

Edges are always the most productive places, places where two (or more) forces interact. Look at a mangrove swamp for example. These are some of the richest environments on earth. By virtually any measure you care to name - resilience of the ecosystem, complexity of plant/animal interactions, absolute number of species and biomass – mangroves come out top. A mangrove swamp is a special ecotone, a place where a number of environments meet. Fresh water meets the sea in a muddy tidal delta, creating deep, current-dragged troughs and shallow pools. Silt, rich in nutrients, carried by rivers from far inland, meets the ocean. Some material sinks to the bottom (depending on the tidal conditions), some creates a nutrient rich scum on the water's surface.

In this halfway world some creatures remain bathed in freshwater, even those who swim out to sea may be carefully following the plumes of river outwash that cascade into the brine. Carefully they follow the flow, invisible to the human eye, of the river as it meanders between the mangrove roots. Other beings from the sea, which are at home in the oceanic world, get to travel with the rhythm of the river, sucked upstream and into the embrace of the land. Then there are others, dilettantes of the between-space, who can move as easily in fresh as salt water, specialised microbes, amphibious creatures and fish who have learnt the value of being able to forage in these two realms.

This mixing alchemical Scorpionic soup of silt and salt and ocean-blown detritus and river water is further mixed with the air as its third key element. Over the mangrove swamp the air hangs thick and sometimes almost static. The lattice of the trees and vines and countless lichens (which droop in huge skeins) serves as a windbreak. From the atmosphere the minute waving of crab claws and the boiling up of bacteria fold the air into the mud. This process enhances the decaying processes that drive the swamp. Beneath the water anaerobic decay releases nutrients for filter feeders and big fish with whiskers and primitive eyes. Above the earth the air is rich in aerobic decay. Flies of a thousand types are generated, and upon them prey a wide variety of birds.

In permaculture (the art and science of designing sustainable systems) this phenomena is known as 'the edge effect'. This is an pattern which it is vital to understand when working with the Earth. To see a clear illustration of this go and have a look at a conventional field, look at where the highest diversity of species exists – it will be at the edge. Look at where the plants are growing most vigorously (even in a field of non-organic grain this still holds true) – it will be the edge. One of the intentions behind the permaculture approach to designing gardens is to maximise this effect. It is for this reason that permaculture plots (be they allotments or full-blown farms) tend to look messy. Like the mangrove swamp they are not about clean and clear edges but rather about mixing elements in such a way that they mutually support one another. Mixing crops, companion planting, using spiral paths that allow maximum access and provide the longest possible edge – these and many other practices are designed to maximise the edge effect. It is at the edges that nutrients collect - that power collects.

Magick is itself one such edge. It is quintessentially the world of the between; between fact and phantasy, between divine and demonic, between reality and imagination, between matter and mind. Magick positions itself in the liminal space – it frequents the temporal autonomous zones (in both physical and virtual cultural spaces). Magick works between the worlds of humanity and of the gods, in the betweeness spaces of midnight, in the threshold world of the 'neither-neither', in states of gnosis where there is no knower and no known.

Magick, then, is the art and science of navigating the liminal space. In social terms magick is the art and science of traversing those zones of change and betweenness that we call birth, puberty, marriage, death and more. All those moments and times in which the human spirit needs to talk itself into reality through ceremony – these are the times when our sense of self is propelled from one existence to another. It is at these times that we hunger for techniques and technologists to help us make those changes. Yes social ritual provides many other functions. It creates categories and shores up the status quo by providing a framework through which the position of an individual in culture can be judged (married/unmarried, baptised/confirmed, student/ graduate). But this should not blind us to the other reasons for the need for social ritual – we need it because in making a transition we need not only to tell others but to find suitable ways of telling ourselves that we are different.

As the pallid hand of Christianity falls from the helm of our society we need new ways, new 'facilitators' and techniques to help us attain these milestones of being with beauty and passion and humour.

In modern English-speaking Paganism the overriding metaphor is that of the wheel of the year. Here the rich edge is explored in ritual that exists between the personal, the social and the bioregional. As the first flowers of spring appear so this process is linked directly to the emergence of a new consciousness in the individual. This process is celebrated on a social level – perhaps at a public 'open' pagan ceremony. It may also be marked by a smaller more personal ritual and celebrated in some way by an activity (going for a walk, having a special meal) that is in some way deliberately connected to the season.

Halloween is one such edge in the wheel of the year. Perhaps *the* edge in that it is, apparently, the last day of the 'old Celtic' year. As the festival of the dead, both in European ancient Pagan culture as much as in Modern Mexican folk custom, Halloween straddles the worlds of the here-and-now and the been-and-gone. It is a time when the dead live, when the veil between the seen and the unseen is compromised.

> In this time that is not a time
> In this place that is not a place
> Between the realm of humans
> And of the Gods

At Halloween autumn's tramp is heavy and one can hear, breathing low behind it, the footfall of the coming winter. The trees flutter the last of their leaves and by the end of November they will be utterly stripped. The grey skull cap of sky might hang monotonously overhead, or else fat black rain clouds announce the first squalls. And sometimes there is clarity in the season. The smell of bonfires peppers the twilight, but the air itself is clear and fresh and crisp.

Of course Halloween is also about fun. It's about plastic devil horns and face painting for kids. It's about the kind of grotesque comedy that sends shivers of excitement and horror through adult and child alike. I remember as a child that I used to call this feeling 'being drunk on night', when you get that crazy nervous energy, that tremulous terror and wide-eyed buzz. Again we are on the edge here. On the edge where the child's giggling could so easily become the tearful babbling of terror. Where, to celebrate the ancestors, we must poke fun at our own mortality by dressing like the dead.

That year our Halloween ritual would be in three parts, each merging and informing the other. One would be a small ritual for a group of us, with some friends, with only myself and my partner confirmed ritualists. The second would be an open ritual, a public ceremony performed by members of The Order of Bards, Ovates and Druids (OBOD). The third was to be a chaos magick session with myself, Brother Kondwani and Brother rhino. This was our Halloween…

## Teenwitch Vampire Horror!

Buffy is our hero. Combining the qualities of vacuous valley girl and destiny-driven saviour of the world she is an awesome creation. On one level she is a woman who is able to walk through a vampire-infested graveyard, at dead of night, without fear. She is thus the desired form, the incarnated wish for freedom of nocturnal movement and of physical strength that so many women crave. She is a nightwalker, a leader and yet still maintains a femininity that, at times, borders on the shallow stereotype of woman. She has great hair, great nails, typically overblown American dress sense and still manages to kick ass!

What a fabulous goddess to invoke!

Sister Artemis and I had worked magick many times before but for Sui and Lexa this was to be a fairly novel experience. We had discussed the basic idea, the key element being that everyone was happy to dress up as and incarnate a character from the series.

The ritual was supposed to be serious but also to be fun. We wanted to enjoy it, to tap into that crazy Halloween lunacy and into the bonding of us as a group of friends that Buffy itself is founded upon. We all knew who we would be. Sister Artemis identified with Willow and would take her post in the West, I would incarnate Giles in the North, Sui would become Xander in the East and Lexa would be Buffy in the fiery south. We dressed appropriately prior to starting the ritual. Lexa put on her make-up, Sui found a flouncey blue shirt and began getting into character with wise cracks. Donning a blazer myself and holding a large magickal tome I started to stutter and crease my brow, trying to imitate Giles as much as I was able.

Before the ritual we had obtained some large balloons and these had been partly filled with flour. Upon these we drew faces, the faces of those things that were our own personal vampires. The things that suck you dry – old worn-out relationships, anxiety and loneliness. Each of us also had a stake, we'd spent the hours prior to the ritual chatting and sharpening them up (Lexa was going to carve upon hers the magickal name 'Mr Pointy' for added authenticity).

Willow cast the circle, walking round the living room using her finger as a wand and we felt the atmosphere change. As easily as diving into a pool we had entered the magickal realm, the liminal space.

I began the ritual, blinking in a Giles like fashion and peering into my Big Magick Book, I spoke the spell;

> Oh mighty spirits,
> Enflame us with your power
> On this Halloween night
> Give us the power
> To walk between the worlds
> To take on these vampires
> Those parts of ourselves and situations
> Which drain us of vitality
> To destroy them!

We each took a slug of tequila, and in turn each of us declared who we were and what we brought to the ritual.

> Xander bringing intelligence, wit, jokes, lies and stories!
> Buffy bringing passion, power and kick ass strength!
> Willow bringing sensitivity, psychic power and care!
> Giles bringing learning, and plain good old-fashioned decency!

Buffy stood, clutching Mr Pointy and holding a balloon vampire by the string attached to it.

Well let's waste these vamps!

'To the graveyard!' we chorused, and dousing the lights and grabbing our stakes and balloons we hurried out the door and into the night.

Outside the vast full moon hung in the sky, illuminating the world with its eerie cold light. In the distance fireworks could be heard. Excitedly, trying to hold it together, we jogged down the hill, stakes and vampire victims in our hands. We crossed the road, which separates the church from a section of graveyard. Here trees and overgrown rose bushes tumbled over the graves. During the previous winter the ground has subsided and so the grass remained uncut and beginning to fill-up with vigorous weeds. We had joked earlier that evening that we might end up falling through the weakened earth and into a subterranean crypt. Now the possibility seemed quite real but rather than create fear, this added to the energy of the ritual. We were all fired up – drunk more on the night itself than the shots of Mexican spirit.

Without any further words we swapped our balloons so that each person was carrying the vampire of another member of the party. Once this was done we ran around the graveyard finding suitable places to secrete the vamps. Then we gathered in the centre of the graveyard by a large ancient marbled tomb.

'Let's get 'em!' cried Buffy and we were off, hunting round the graveyard, running carelessly over the long grass, dodging behind tombstones and generally behaving like teenagers. As Giles I attempted to retain a little more gravitas but, given the atmosphere of the event, found this impossible. And so, shrieking and giggling I began my search, looking for the characteristic spheroid energy field that indicates the presence of major vampire action.

Finally I spotted it, beneath a low thorn tree. Hanging almost motionless in the dark, its eyes filled with moonlight, its fangs apparent. This was the vampire of fear of incompetence. It was the vampire that makes you worry so much about not being able to do a thing that you do invariably fail. It was the vampire that makes you spend so much time worrying about what can go wrong that you forget to build up a picture of success (a generally more fruitful approach). Whether you're dealing with taking a driving test or doing a presentation to the board of directors, it's this vampire that stands in your way. That stands in my way – and there it was grinning, hanging from a tree.

With a yell I went for it, gripping my stake with both hands I plunged through the moonlit night towards the vampire. The wooden point found its mark and the vampire was hit! Just like on the TV as the balloon popped the white flour showered out, leaving a cloud of dust hanging momentarily in the air before falling to earth.

For me the hunt was over and so I walked back to the marble tomb. Willow and Xander returned soon afterwards from their own successful missions. But Buffy seemed to have made a wide circle round the graveyard, perhaps enjoying her freedom to move in the night, armed and dangerous, intoxicated with the hero archetype. Then we saw her, running across the grass very fast and I realised that her vampire was right next to us. Hanging from a young sycamore tree, it's grotesque face washed with moonlight. Buffy cried out and raised Mr Pointy high above her head, jumping to reach her target, and the vampire was killed – vanishing in a puff of dust. We cheered at what was, when all said and done, was a pretty neat bit of bad guy despatchment.

We returned to the house and closed the temple. Each of us thanked the powers of the elements and Sister Artemis uncast the circle. Our Buffy ritual was done.

## Druid Death Cult

From a small circle of friends the circle widens outward. The next day was to be the OBOD open Samhain ceremony. Since the weather was uncertain the location would be a tree-screened green near the car park which is at the foot of the Long Man of Wilmington. Rituals in the warmer part of the year tended to be held in the small hill directly beneath the Long Man. But for this Samhain rite the little green was perfect. A few thorn trees dotted the spot, and in the distance the Long Man, that enigmatic sigil of Sussex, looked on.

As with many of the major celebrations there was a fairly large number of people present. I arrived with Sister Artemis and a couple of good friends including Peter who was then ten years old. The beauty of Pagan forms such as Druidry is that the outer edges of the movement are so visible, open and inclusive. There are plenty of more challenging and secretive elements in Druidry but open rituals allow a wide variety of people to come into contact, often for the first time, with practical earth-centred spirituality. Unsurprisingly (though often forgotten by old hands) a simple open ritual can be a profound, life changing experience for somebody, if the whole thing is new territory.

People gradually assembled including the chosen Chief of the OBOD. A number of people had brought pumpkins that would be used to make a simple altar in the centre of the circle. Others had brought apples, nuts and drink to share in the ceremony. The early afternoon was clear but with the unmistakable autumn scent of wet and decay on it.

There were no other children present (except a couple of babes in arms) and Peter was getting bored. It became obvious that he would rather not stand in the circle and take part. His mum suggested that she sit out the ceremony and go with him to the excellent nearby pub (The Giant's Rest) for lemonade and crisps. Although an experienced solitary witch, Peter's mum had never experienced an open Druid ritual before so, rather than her miss out, I opted to take Peter to the pub. So, as the assembled company prepared to join hands and remember the beloved dead, Peter and I wandered off in search of child-friendly drinks and cake.

Although Druid open rituals are fairly gentle affairs I had been looking forward to the ceremony so, to begin with, I was a bit cross. I wanted Peter's mum to experience the ceremony, and appreciated that Peter just couldn't fit in. Although not unfamiliar with the ideas of Paganism or ritual (all children understand ritual as a general practice – try snuffing out birthday candles rather than blowing them and see if they object) Peter just couldn't get comfortable. He was really bored, that often heard complaint of youth, which is perfectly true. When you have little autonomy, when you understand about money but don't have much of your own, when you need the support of adults but cannot yet be a full part of their world, boredom must inevitably strike. Being ten is perhaps particularly tricky. You're not really a child anymore, not able to simply draw or play, or babble endlessly. But neither yet have you got the teenager's awkward attempts at coolness or opportunities to create a new culture away from the generation above. Beginning to develop sexuality but not yet able to focus on the concrete worries of spots and genital hair – you are in-between, lost in a liminal space that only time will mend.

So Peter and I walked down the road, past the huge and ancient yew tree in the Wilmington churchyard and into the pub. They had just stopped serving food so all we could get to eat was cake, a fact that disappointed Peter not one bit. He with his orange and me with a pint of bitter we decided that it was still warm enough to sit outside and so we found a trestle table and sat down.

'Is it nice?' I asked Peter indicating his cake.

'humm – I think ghosts feel the same as the wind'

Part of the fun of kids is not knowing where their minds are, sometimes it's so like talking to someone on acid that it's quite untrue.

'Yeah?'

'Maybe when you die your spirit just turns into wind. Maybe it just floats out when you breathe your last breath.'

I considered this. Okay it was Halloween, discussing death was certainly on the menu and I'd seen my grandmother die in March of that year so had spent (more than usual) time thinking about human mortality.

'I think you have an eternal moment' I said, 'I think that when you die you have a last thought that seems to go on for ever – like a dream.'

'Uh?'

'The way that a dream is only a dream after you wake up, and then you call it a dream but at the time you don't think you're dreaming, you just dream'.

'Yes,' acknowledged Peter, 'sometimes I dream I'm going out of my body, flying up. Sometimes I think that maybe when you die you go flying up.'

'Lots of people say they feel like they are flying when they die.'

'How can we know?' asked Peter.

'Well I mean people who die, so their heart stops, maybe if they are in an accident, but then their heart is started again.'

'By pressing, Aaggh!' Peter clasped his hands to his chest mimicking heart massage and sticking his tongue out.

'Yeah. Sometimes people who have died say they see a tunnel and a light.'

'But what happens afterwards. What happens to YOU if you don't get made alive again?'

'Well different people believe different things.'

(Rolling his eyes to indicate that I'd said the bleeding obvious)

'Yeah like your soul or spirit goes into an animal, or another person - a baby. Or that you go to heaven – ugh.'

I could tell that Peter's conception of heaven probably involved lots of angels and harps and little that he considered worthwhile.

'Maybe part of you goes into the wind' I replied, 'like you said. Maybe part of you becomes a ghost and another part of you gets reincarnated.'. I've always liked systems in which you get to have your cake and eat it. In ancient Egyptian culture after death different aspects of the Self get to do different things; one part remains on earth and gently fades away like a ghost, one part goes on to live in a heavenly reality which looks very much like earthy reality, and another element goes back to the big pool of universal life force and eventually ends up in a another being.

Peter considered this, 'maybe your ghost only lasts for a while, like an echo'.

I sipped my pint.

'Maybe when people forget you your ghost just blows away. Do you think it is scary?'

'What death? Dying? Yes I think in some ways it is. I think sometimes it's sad'

'But maybe dying is okay, just becoming a spirit – you could go wherever you wanted. Even through walls!'

Imagination is the stuff that forms the bridge from one world to another. Magick is the technology of forging the imagination to carry our sense of self from one world to another. For Peter his imagination will help carry him from child to adult but this does not only come from developing a picture of your self as a grown-up. It comes by imagining and developing a full ontology, a full way of thinking about the world. This includes a notion of death, or perhaps more importantly, what happens to you after death. For Peter death represented the possibility of freedom and wasn't tied to ideas of terror or pain. This is as it should be. When you're ten you are immortal. You don't know what you don't know (which is good because if you knew all that you don't know you'd be crushed by this knowledge). Your body is still expanding and growing and rising up from the unconscious, the continent of sexuality is surfacing. What you lack in autonomy a loved and cared for child (such as Peter) makes up for in joy at the possibilities of the world, the possibility of freedom.

## Suicide PACT

The temple was prepared with the insignia of Samhain – cauldron, peacock feathers, pumpkin lanterns and skulls. We burnt opoponax until the room was thick with smoke.

Three figures, clothed in black robes were silent for a moment. This is one of the key parts of any ritual – the breath that stops the world. That kills the disorganised chaos of thought and care about past and future. The door is bolted, the telephone disconnected, there is only this space and it is the whole universe, only this time and it is all eternity. There is nothing, there is nothing but this.

We began by intoning the IAO formula. Brother Kondwani and Brother rhino then sat motionless and began to chant the name of the Great Goddess of this time He-Ka-Tay,

> He-Ka-Tay
> He-Ka-Tay
> He-Ka-Tay
> He-Ka-Tay
> He-Ka-Tay
> He-Ka-Tay
> He-Ka-Tay...

I heaped incense on the coals, sending the delicious perfume spiralling upwards and called:

I invoke you, beloved Hekate of the Crossroads and the Three
Ways
Saffron-cloaked Goddess of the Heavens, the Underworld
and the Sea
Tomb-frequenter, mystery-raving with the souls of the dead
Daughter of Perses, Lover of the Wilderness who exults among
deer
Nightgoing One, Protectress of dogs, Unconquerable Queen
Beast-roarer, Dishevelled One of compelling countenance
Tauropolos, Keyholding Mistress of the whole world
Ruler, Nymph, Mountain-wandering Nurturer of youth
Maiden, I beg you to be present at these sacred rites
Ever with a gladsome heart and every gracious to the Oxherd.

O Three-faced Selene, come to me beloved mistress
Graciously hear my sacred spells;
Image of Night, Youthful One,
Dawn-born lightbringer to mortals
Who rides upon fierce-eyed bulls,
O Queen, you who drive your chariot
On equal course with Helios,
You dance with the triple forms of the triple Graces
As you revel with stars.
You are Justice and the thread of the Fates,
Clotho, Lachesis and Atropos,
O Three-headed One you are
Persephone, Megaira and Allecto
O one of many shapes who arms your hands
With terrible dark-glowing lamps,
Who shakes locks of fearsome serpents at your brow,
Whose mouths send forth the roar of bulls,
Whose womb is thick with reptile-scales,
At whose shoulders are rows of venomous serpents,
Bound across your back beneath murderous chains.

O Night-bellower, Lover of solitude, Bull-faced and Bull-
headed One
You have the eyes of bulls and the voice of dogs.

Your forms are hidden in the legs of lions.
Your ankle is wolf-shaped, and savage dogs are friendly to you,
Wherefore they call you Hekate, Many-named, Mente,
Cleaving the air like arrow-shooting Artemis.
O Goddess of Four faces, Four names, Four ways,
Artemis, Persephone, Deer-shooter, night-shiner,
Thrice-resounding, Triple-voiced, Three-headed, Thrice-named Selene
O Trident-bearing One, of Three-faces, Three necks, Three ways,
Who holds undying flaming life in triple baskets.
You frequent the Three-ways and are Mistress of the Three Decads.
Be gracious unto me who is invoking you and hearken favourably.

You encompass the vast world of night,
You make the Daemons shudder and the immortals tremble,
O Many-named Goddess who brings glory to men,
Whose children are fair, O bull-eyed One, Horned One,
Nature, All-mother, who brings forth both Gods and men,
You roam around Olympus and traverse the wide and fathomless Abyss,
You are the Beginning and the End, and you alone are Mistress of All:
For from you are All things, and in you, Eternal One, do all things end.
You bear at your brow an everlasting diadem,
The unbreakable and irremovable bonds of the great Kronos,
And you hold in your hands a golden sceptre
Which is encircled by a formula inscribed by Kronos himself
Who gave it you to bear in order that all things remain steadfast:
*Overpowerer and Overpowered One*
*Conqueror of men and Damnodamia.*
You rule Chaos *Araracharara ephthiskere*,
Hail Goddess and attend your epithets.

I offer you this incense Child of Zeus

Arrow-shooter, Heavenly One, Goddess of Harbours,
Mountain-roamer, Goddess of the Crossroads,
Nocturnal One of the Underworld, Shadowy One of Hades,
Still One who frightens, having a feast among the graves.
You are Night, Darkness and broad chaos,
For you are Necessity hard to escape.

You are Fate, you are Erinys and the Torture,
You are the Murderess and Justice
You hold Cerberus in chains,
You are steely-blue with serpent-scales,
O serpent-haired and Serpent-girdled One,
Blood-drinker, Death-bringer who breeds corruption,
Feaster on hearts, Flesh-eater who devours those who died
before their time,
Grave-resounder, Driver to the Wanderings of Madness,
Come to my sacrifices and fulfil this task for me.[12]

The Goddess of the Dark was with us. We were each wrapped in the sooty blackness of her cloak. The air was thick, strange, suffused with the eldritch aura of the Queen of the Crossroads.

We lay down and I started the tape – the pathworking which I have called 'Journey to the Death Star'.

Living in the post-post modern condition we have no single myth but a polymorphous production of many stories, many discourses. The intention of this pathworking was to allow each participant to create a clear model of their own death. A model which incorporates specific images (walking into the light) and which reinforces the perception of one's own death as the reward, the culmination and climax of one's life. Rather than viewing one's death as the inevitable and tawdry postscript of one's story it is the pinnacle of achievement. To have a good death, which for me would be the ability to relax and enter death consciously and with acceptance, is the key to one's life.

When we die, I believe, we have the chance of a moment of infinite being. As the neural circuits of the brain shut down, starved of oxygen, the deeply rooted programs of our first experience re-emerge and we are again conscious of this, the lowest stratum of thought. This process is paralleled by what happens when you start destroying a complex neural network computer, though they have disappeared from sight, as we obliterate sections of the network the basic training programs used to set-up the system return. Perhaps this is the basis for the memory of seeing one's life flash before your eyes following severe trauma.

I believe (for the moment) that in the last few tenths of a second before consciousness winks out of existence we can apprehend the fact that 'I'm dying', and that, if we can relax into this, we can find a moment of total bliss, of ecstasy – heaven. That moment is like the numinous peak that comes at the height of an acid trip, the singularity where all things are one and the world of Maya, of discrete objects, becomes fused into one bliss wave of being. Unlike the peak of the psychedelic process there is no come-down, no afterwards and no dis-integrated consciousness that re-emerges from the event that can 'compare' the divine unity with now – because you're dead. Like dreams, we only call the dream such after dreaming itself has ceased – in the case of death, for our individual consciousness there is no 'after'. (This view does not inherently disallow paradigms that suggest the continuity of consciousness after the brain is dead, it may simply be a different aspect of consciousness that ends up being reincarnated or becoming a discarnate spirit – especially if we read consciousness as a multiplicity of selves).

The pathworking began in the usual way, relaxing the body, stilling the mind, focusing on the breath and its flow. But went beyond this...

> The world of the dead and of the living interpenetrate tonight - the shadow realm of the un-manifest and the forgotten, the living world of manifestation and memory. Tonight the pathway of time knits together these two worlds, the veil is thinner - listen...

> Imagine your history, your own timeline, your songline, like a coffin path across the autumn landscape. The path cuts through the dark, marked by candles or lights, past the ancient trees, down the secret valleys of experience, across the borders of knowledge. The path crosses the zone between the living and the dead, between phantasy and reality, and as you follow it you

know that you are within the fairy realm, the liminal space of this Halloween night.

Follow your path, your destiny, as you walk in spirit vision be aware of your body here on the ground in this temple and know that it is safe and healthy and well, and that your spirit body is making a great journey - the journey of your dying - your final magick. Know that what you feel in your physical body is 'as if' and need not concern your earthly skin - not now, not yet - as you Will.

Now as you follow the coffin path of your own death across the landscape you become aware of a star, hanging above the road you are travelling.

This star is your death - it is the totem of your material being, your mortality. It is the signal of your journey's end, and the compass by which you can chart the course of your incarnation - your destiny and your greatest blessing.

As you watch the star growing feel your spirit body moving forward in time, moving along your path toward the star, collapsing time until your are near the star which is the inevitable moment of your own death.

Feel the sensations of your spirit body, your skeleton, the bones old and tired now relaxing, no longer needing to fight gravity. Your spine unlocking from tension and resting, crumbling, your finger bones resting in peace, immobile. Feel your muscles uncurl, relax, slacken and drop, without tone or tension, without effort of need to fight. Feel your nervous system, the billion scintillating impulses within you. Feel how they are stuttering, cutting out, first a few, then more and more. Tingles in your fingers and toes as your nervous system begins to shut down.

Feel the flow of your blood, the sound of it pumping in your ears, your breathing becoming shallower as your death approaches.

And as this happens let your mind begin to focus away from your body, but remain conscious of its processes, feel your body shutting down, sleeping, dying, be aware of and welcome each sensation and the creeping disconnection of your mind and body. Feel your heart still weakly pumping, nervous energy in your body discharging, coming to earth and stopping.

Let your dying dream come upon you, feel how it will be to die, let your mind drift away from your body, lying crumpled and worn on the coffin path. Drift up towards the star of your death, your escaton. Your last few, shallow breaths are happening now, let your bodymind enjoy them, let your dream of dying, your own myth guide you, travel towards that star, the strange attractor of your Kia, the flaming centre of your True Will - let the edges between the worlds collapse - breath out for the last time and enter your dream of dying.

Die.
And when your living body demands it - breath again! Bring the dream of your death back into your life now, let your timeline expand and let the image of the star of your dying fade, breath deeply and feel the life of the universe within you, be returned to this world, to this night. Bring with you the memory of your dying dream to comfort you when your death comes in this world and as an ally creating pleasure, freedom and power. Breathe and be alive.

For Brother rhino his death-star begins in an accident and emergency unit, the shouting of nurses and doctors, the blood, the panic gives way to the light and he is dragged up through the ceiling...

For all of us we enter the star, the doorway to death. We have felt how it is to die, and our imagination has framed, has begun to form a personal interpretation of 'what happens when you die – how does it feel?'

We each enter the star as we breath out our last breaths…relinquishing all attachments, all division between self and other, all being. There is only the ecstasy of the collapsing of all boundaries. The gravitation of love overwhelms all elements in reality, fusing them in one brilliant star, a perfect moment that lasts for eternity…

> … breath in, breath in the truth of your life NOW, breath in the fact that you are alive NOW but that you have a myth, a death story that opens into this amazing final reality. Feel your body healthy and vigorous, sit up and be awake!

And banish with laughter.

Halloween being a time of the inward spiral, of catabolic energy, we then undertook another pathworking. This time the design of Brother Kondwani, we are taken back through our cellular memory, back to our single celled heritage, back to Eden. Then we return to now, through the eight circuits model of being, activating and exploring each circuit as we do.

And from this Brother rhino led us through the final meditation. In these days of high-octane gnosis with explosives, exotic hallucinogens and electronic methods of trance induction, one should not forget the power of listening with one-pointedness to a sacred text.

> Life's Impermanence

> Once acquired, this precious life with liberty and opportunity
> Has the characteristics of instantaneity, impermanence, and decay.
> The three realms are deceptive and illusory in nature.
> Though beautiful by the wealth of its four continents,
> Our earthly environment is impermanent and exhibits decay.

> Even this body should be recognised as a ball of foam,
> Like those of all these beings now on earth.
> In a hundred years, they will certainly not be,
> Since everything born eventually dies.

Just as your own life span will come to an end,
In places like markets, crossroads, guest houses,
All these crowds of diverse beings will be scattered.

Contemplate the certainty from the heart that your relations
And the resources of your amassed possessions,
Like a city deserted, will come to nothing.
Since whatever wealth one has amassed
Is impermanent and without essence, you should be detached;
You ascend to the wealthy cities of paradise,
Even as you go beyond death and fall to miserable lives.

Be sure that pride in this life or wealth grants no equanimity,
Since one is separated in time from things outer and inner.
Since both impermanence and death are certain,
Give up on the delusion of permanence.

Subatomic matter endures momentarily,
Being impermanent as a flash of lightning,
So you should realise ultimate truth just as quickly,
The variety of habitats and life-forms is transient,
Essenceless as an illusion or a banana tree,
Therefore this life-cycle is called impermanent,
And clinging to one's self or work is not acceptable.[13]

My birthday falls on November 1st and it was on that date that the wheel of re-birth turned again. My partner told me that she was pregnant and I wept with joy.

Through the magick of gestation, of organic time,
Rooted in the Muladhara, the world of bodily form,
Emerging from death, the possibility of new life.
The alpha and omega that leads me through the world.
My story is thus enchanted.

Now that's what I call Chaos Magick.

# Key Resources

## Texts

*Saravá! Afro-Brazilian Magick*, Carol L. Dow. Llewellyn 1997
*The Handbook of Yoruba Religious Concepts*,      Baba Ifa Karade
Weiser 1994
*Macumba*, A.J. Langguth, Harper and Row 1975
*Pomba Gira: The Formidable Female Messenger of the Gods*, Antonio
*Teixeira Alves Neto*, Technicians of the Sacred 1990
*Kali*, Elizabeth U. Harding, Nicolas Hays 1993
*Liber Null & Psychonaut*, Pete Carroll, Weiser 1987
*Maat Magick*, Nema, Weiser 1995
*Mystical Qabalah*, Dion Fortune, Weiser 2000
*Prime Chaos*, Phil Hine, New Falcon 1999
*The Lens of Perception*, Hal Zina Bennett, Celestial Arts 1994
*The Goddess Hekate*, Stephen Ronan (Ed), Chthonios Books 1992

## Websites

www.rootswithoutend.com
www.awostudycenter.com
www.asemarabo.com
www.slivoski.com/angels/prayer3.htm
www.phhine.ndirect.co.uk
www.indifference.demon.co.uk/fotamecus
www.spiralnature.com/magick/rituals/fotempower.html
www.web-alive.com/dm/index.html
www.occultebooks.com

## Sounds

*Enjoy the Chaos*, Ozomatli
*Jehovahkill*, Julian Cope
*Rock Action*, Mogwai
*Pagan Dance*, Mother Destruction
*White Rose Live*, Mother Destruction
*The Diver in the Cave*, Philip Sheppard
Various currently unreleased material by Sui Said Love  MP3 @
www.suisaidlove.com

# Volume 2

## Introduction

'You can have any colour you want, as long as it's black' – Henry Ford.

Chaos Magick is a paradox. The very term itself is proposing to direct the disorder of the universe towards a specified, ordered goal. Bearing this in mind therefore, I propose you read the following work and allow it to sink into your mind in its own time. Suspend your disbelief in magick when reading it in order to squeeze the most enjoyment from it. In a world as chaotic and disordered as ours enjoyment is a rare gift, so do not squander it when it is presented to you on a platter.

At its best I find the Chaos Magick current of esoteric thought so broad as to appeal to anyone regardless of cultural and religious boundaries. It allows you to believe anything you want, because at the root of all mankinds various ideas, philosophies and doctrines is the realisation that magick, mystery and the unknown exist regardless of belief. If you stripped away all ideas, thoughts, religions, theories and doctrines, you would still have magick, mystery and the unknown. They are fundamental to our existence, and how we deal with them defines who we are. I believe Chaos Magick shows us the way to deal with these things on our own terms. It attempts to free us from the control of others. The gurus, the advertising executives, the politicians, the vicars, the priests and the schoolteachers are all in one sense magicians, trying to control our thoughts and actions using the methods of mind control we all take for granted. Repetition and emotional trauma are their techniques. Chaos magick reclaims these techniques for ourselves allowing us to indoctrinate ourselves and see the world through our own eyes for the first time.

I find Chaos Magick an intensely personal philosophy. Its techniques are to be experienced directly rather than theorised over, and through them a world begins to appear which no one else has ever experienced. It is unique to you, and this can be a very scary prospect. In such a world there are no signposts to show you the way and no policemen to question about which direction to take. You have become an explorer in this world, forging new paths into the unknown. You need to find your own solutions to the particular problems you encounter, and you need to be ruthlessly honest with yourself about results (what worked for you and what didn't?) because these are the only maps you have to help navigation in the future. It is important that you do begin to explore this brave new world however, as this is the only way that everyone can approach a way to get everything they want. An ideal very close to my heart.

All the belief systems of the world have particular myths, or stories associated with them. These sacred texts transmit the core spiritual knowledge of that system of thought through the use of metaphor. Chaos Magick has no sacred texts and I believe locked inside each individual practitioners life experience (past, present and future) lies all the knowledge needed to create (and ultimately live) these myths for ourselves. Hopefully, this volume gives each reader the various clues, methods, examples and techniques towards creating their own myths. These are the keys with which to unlock the secret knowledge held within.

It is easy to describe experience as something that happens to your self, but what does this mean? What is this 'self' people refer to? There is never one single self that performs acts of creativity and magick. All acts of creativity are collaboration between different people, ideas and the world around. The self could simply be described as the one who compiles these various ingredients and seasons them in such a way as to create something different. A new dish to taste and present to the world. Then this dish in turn may be used by some other self to compile another recipe. Bear this in mind when reading this volume. Use any elements that take your fancy and produce your own recipes, but always let the world know where you got your ingredients!

The following volume of this book is separated into three acts.

*Act I: Abstract* is the telling of a personal journey I undertook during my training in Chaos Magick. It is the end product of three years of magical work. It is written as truthfully as I can relate the experience of those events. It is important I mention this, as Chaos Magick is a path that leads ultimately to the integration of magic within your life. Therefore the boundary of what is fact and fiction becomes ever changing both on a personal level and a cultural one. All we as authors can do when talking about experiences within Chaos is give you our snapshot of a particular time and place.

*Act II: Theory* gives an introduction to the theory behind some of the key themes related in Act I. I make no special claims to the theory expounded in this act, you can take it with as much salt as you wish. However, if you allow it to, the theory lets you deeper into the belief system and will increase your magical ability if understood. An understanding of Act II will also increase your understanding and enjoyment of the narrative in Act I. All you need do is suspend your present beliefs long enough to let the story work its magic.

*Act III: Practicum* is a series of practical exercises for you to follow. Performing these exercises is the only true way to understand Acts I and II, and I suggest you do them in the order they are presented. They take you deep down the rabbit hole of Chaos Magick, if they are performed correctly. I don't want to hear any critics ringing me up to harangue me about how bad this book is until they have done the exercises. Only then will I welcome, or appreciate, people's opinions because only then will they be able to tell the story of their past, present and future; and stories are my greatest passion.

Throughout the volume it should be noted that the views and prejudices expressed are mine alone. From everything said about Chaos Magick in this introduction it would be stupid to assume they are the expressed opinion of the various individuals who make up the Chaos Magick current.

Greg Humphries – Bristol, June 2002.

# Act I: Abstract

How does a tale begin?

Well a good starting point for this one would be with a confession.
I am a magician.

Don't mistake this book for a gratuitous work of fiction, it isn't. It's a confessional account of why I consider myself a worthwhile human being, yet have just killed something I love so dearly I consider it my own child. I'm sat here writing this in Buckinghamshire and it's the 16th January 2002. Considering the act of sacrilege just performed I am feeling remarkably happy and calm, the smell of sandalwood incense fills my nostrils and the saliva in my mouth has the metallic tang of mercury. Having finally rid this earth of the child's body I feel as if a weight has been lifted from my shoulders. A responsibility of unmanageable proportions has been released. My wife and I colluded in its death, we both lit the fires that eventually burnt its body without a trace. No police force or jury will catch us, or hold us, or sit over us and pass judgement, for we conceived and raised the child in secret, feeding and caring for it for two years. We gave it love and attention worthy of a King, making it fit and healthy enough to pass from the world of dreams and imagination it inhabited, to another of utter reality.

So, dear reader read on, and become one of the growing jury at our trial. Yet, only give your verdict when you have heard the whole story, lest having read it you decide to follow in our murderous footsteps. My wife and I shall both live with the consequences of our actions. As I said, do not make the mistake of thinking this a work of fiction, we created a child and after two years of loving attention we killed it. By telling you the truth, the whole truth and nothing but the truth about my journey which led to this act of sacrifice, I hope to present my case. So help me God.

I love my child, and I know that one day we shall be reunited.

The origins of the path, which was to end in the flames of this funeral pyre, can be traced back to a hot August day in 1999. We had walked for miles across the Wiltshire downs to hear the storyteller relate the tale of Wayland the Smith. We all sat together on the long barrow encircled by the beeches in that ancient place which held so many stories. Magically the storyteller captured our attention, and led us far across the sea to a different time and place. He told us of the brothers, Slagfid, Egil and Wayland who one day met the resting, swan-like Valkyries near their home. How they fell in love, married and lost their brides to the excitement of Valhalla. How softly spoken Wayland stayed at home, longing for his wife's return and forged a ring for each day he waited. How those rings enmeshed him within the pride and arrogance of King Nidud and his sons. How Nidud cut the sinews of Wayland's knees so that he may never leave his service, and how Wayland made beautiful, mechanical wings of swan feathers, had his revenge and escaped. The over-riding memory I have of this telling was the closing sentence.

'And then Wayland flew on his wings over the North Sea searching for his bride. Setting up forge here, at Waylands Smithy'.

This set me to thinking about the link between people and their Gods. I realised that the Gods move not on wings, but in the stories and tales of the people who tell them. As the people migrate from place to place the stories move with them. As time advances, cultures change. And as cultures change, so do the Gods. After all, the Gods only exist in stories, don't they?

## The Child Is Conceived

Move with me now on swan-feathered wings to Bristol late October 2000.

I cast my eyes over the Bristol cityscape beyond the kitchen window. A great cumulus raincloud, casting a shadow from the suspension bridge to Cabot's Tower reminding me of Cornwall during the Solar eclipse of 1999. In that summer, three miles south of Falmouth, we experienced the shadow of the moon passing over us, and through us. A portal being created between Bristol October 2000 and Cornwall 1999 as both the shadows passed over us simultaneously. A link created between magical acts. Another host of desires focused from Beyond, and brought through the imagination to Consensus Reality. Another Nexus Point where the synchronicity lay waiting to be recognised and from which Rachel and I decided to make our dreams come true.

The problem with desires is not making them come true, but which desire do you decide on in the first place? How do you know it's what you are going to want in one, two or ten year's time? I would suggest that there is a part of you, hidden behind lots and lots of masks that already knows. It looks at you from very deep, and unknown to your waking mind it guides you. It is Dream, it is your True Will, it is your ineffable Self. And you can only express its wishes when you don't think about it.

And this is where it all starts to get a bit complicated.

We assemble the tools of our trade, we are artists of the unknown. The paper and pens, the paint and tissue paper, the glue and water are all to hand. We stand on the red lino and look at each other as we spill our unconscious onto the paper.

The hands and eyes move with ease a rushing adrenaline flow of energy followed by floating sensations a mark here a Beauty splash of colour there a wave or a pirate ship Honesty money and houses by the sea Love expanding and contracting with phenomenal force Freedom concentrate on the fulcrum of desire neither – neither lies beyond good and evil within the jaws of the Creativity serpent at the gates of wisdom swallowing its own tail red for energy and blue for wealth green for love of You and yellow for Me orange for the clarity that comes with communication and purple for the passion of sex the black stillness of death and that colour from the inside of a sea-shell washed up on a beach the petrol on water all drift onto the paper as if born out of darkness. Happiness.

And then return. Rachel, Vanya and I sit in the kitchen, looking down on the picture we have just created. A huge, colourful masterpiece of semi-automatic art. Our desires are before our very eyes and the task ahead is to try to translate them into something we can work with. A simplified picture we can easily remember. A glyph to be the focus of our energy and love, representing the world we are to inhabit. Our dreams come true, and in our world of dreams everyone gets everything they want. Oh, such utopias on a sheet of A1 paper! Don't rush it. Let it settle in. We leave the picture on the table to dry, the smell of paint and glue dripping onto the floor evoking memories of childhood play and playgroup art lessons.

We return the following day, mugs of coffee in hand, to look on this work of art with a critical eye. No longer the free flowing cup of no-thought, this is the sword of clarity we wield. We lay the tracing paper over the picture and we each in turn draw lines that stand out through the frosted skin. Once we are content we place another piece of tracing paper over the first, and select lines that mean something to us. We see the glyph taking shape before our eyes, until its shape becomes obvious. We can't understand why we didn't see it before. It is obvious. It has always been there, and will always be. The glyph is drawn. A seed to nurture, tend and grow. A precious and beautiful thing has been born. Our dreams condensed into a small perfectly formed picture. The picture is the glyph, is the body of our child and our child is the plan.

# The Light At The End Of The Tunnel

*'For the time being, the monster wasn't in Ricky's closet. For the time being.'* – The Far Side.

Why would you want a child in the first place? You'll only produce another version of yourself. Despite your best intentions the child will grow with your own prejudices and desires imprinting its personality, until one day it realises what you have done and rebels against you. Railing against everything you stand for and turning its back on you, hating you for what you have done. The Fundamentalist Christian sects are full of the sons and daughters of libertine parents, and it seems inevitable there will forever be this backlash effect. How depressing!

There is however a deeper drive to wanting children. Part of me believes the hope of the world is with them, a chance to turn away from the problems of the past and glimpse a bright new, shiny and exciting future. The belief that they might just get it right where we all failed, that we could help them to find the nugget of divine gold in the scrapheap of dull, leaden life. How ideal and twee that seems in this cynical world. And how arrogant to my unbelieving ears, yet still there is a part of me that knows it could be true.

Maybe we cannot do it for the whole of human-kind, an idea too monumental and mind shattering to contain, but we can do it for our own child. We cannot help but imprint it with our own dreams and fears, and all we can hope is that they are the very best dreams and fears we can muster. If the intent is to nurture, and the guidance we have to impart is given with love, then maybe our children will not rampage after us with the bloody spears and blades 'come the teenage revolution'. Perhaps we will have imprinted compassion, empathy and understanding sufficiently that they will forgive us our shortcomings and instead of cutting us off will put us out to pasture instead.

If the guidance we give our children corresponds with the desires of our highest self then how can that guidance fail to be the best we can give?

How to start such a grandiose work? I realise it begins with a question.

Who am I?

Quickly followed by another.

Why am I?

I enter the temple room within my house with these questions in my mind. I exercise for about 30 minutes to shake off the tensions of my day in the office, then I sit down to clear my mind of all conscious thought. Rising up from the depths comes the realisation/memory that these were questions I first asked a long time ago.

I was seventeen years old and studying for my 'A' Level examinations. My parents had the wisdom and foresight to shove me through my second driving test, and I had passed. I had learned to hate the comprehensive school system I knew I was about to leave. I did not hate the other kids, I had some good friends and after all we were all in the same boat. I did not hate the teachers (although I hated their lazy, laconic complicity in the whole thing). No, I hated the system of education itself. It made me angry that the system prepared you for one thing, and one thing only. Work.

A typical day would be as follows, we would all trudge to school ready for an 08.30 am start, we would sit and take orders for a couple of hours before a fifteen minute break. In which we had to avoid conflict with our fellow workers, whilst pretending we were enjoying ourselves. Then back in the classroom for another couple of hours of work; then lunch which to me seemed a longer spell of 'learning to get on' with others I had little in common. This sorry, laborious drudgery continued in the afternoon whilst you constantly watched the minutes tick by until home time.

Remind you of anything? Sat in your office chair, or working in the factory. The commute to your place of work? The clocking on and off? The forced 'getting on' with your boss or co-workers for the good of your career? School seems to me to be a very clever indoctrination process, which sets us up for a life chained to a Protestant Work Ethic. And it's this indoctrination process that I was angry at even then. I didn't know that's why I had a boiling hatred of it at the time, but I knew it was wrong.

Well, that's how it seemed to me anyway. If you disagree, then I hope the system set you up for a life of happiness. After all that's what an education is supposed to do isn't it? Give you freedom and choices, enabling you to be happy. Of course it is; but it didn't do it for me.

That is why, at the age of 17, I drove myself to Clumber Park in Nottinghamshire one night, under the pretence that it would 'help me revise'. I parked on the grass in a clearing among the small silver birches, and turned off the car headlights. I got out the car and lit a cigarette. I looked up at the stars, hanging in the inky blackness above, and shouted at the top of my lungs…

'Who am IIIIIIIIIIIIIIIIII?'

then,

'Wwwwwwwwwwwwwhhhhhhhhhhhhhhhhhhhhhhyyyyyyyyyyyyyyyyyyyyyy?'.

I started to cry, the tension releasing and falling away with the tears. I had asked the question of the night sky, and waited for a reply.

Soon after this moment I scraped through to a place at University (pushed by my parents again, God thank them!) where I began to get interested in the occult and magic.

As I return to myself in the temple, I have a sense of my magical work as a continuous process becoming a bigger and bigger part of my life. A silver thread, which I had picked up at that moment many years ago, and had been following ever since. I think we can view our Holy Guardian Angels as that which wants to make our lives better. It cares about who we are and where we are going. For me it is the beauty at the end of the silver thread. Sometimes, I can enter trance states where I realise the thread is part of that beauty, and the thread is also a part of me; but mainly I keep hold of it, grit my teeth and keep walking. What I want our child to show us on a magical level is how to get Rachel, Vanya and me beyond the gritted teeth of that bloody Protestant Work Ethic, and show us the journey can be just as beautiful as the end result. And if the journey is just as beautiful as the end, then what is the difference between them?

## Is It My Turn To Feed The Baby?

The months pass and we continue to live apart. The M4 motorway between Bristol and London becomes a conduit of longing and desire for us to travel along. The miles pass from conscious awareness and into a liminal realm, the world between Rachel and I. This becomes the world where plans are made and lessons learned.

As the months pass we feed our child more and more. Each time we make love, Rach and I pour energy into its glyph, building his energy. We nurture our baby, who is getting big, and strong. Our child speaks, and begins to let us know what he needs to help him grow. A walk in the country one day, a visit to the beach and a surf the next. Art galleries and libraries, painting and writing. We teach him through our experiences, and our child keeps pushing us towards experiences we enjoy.

Winter has turned into spring, spring passed into summer and we need to ensure the enormous energies generated by the feeding of our baby are being directed by our Holy Guardian Angels. Only with this certainty can we be sure our child is to grow into a world dictated by our highest wishes.

August comes, and I fly to New York to meet some fellow psychonauts at a conference to be held upstate. People arrive from around the world to sweltering heatwave temperatures. As the week progresses rituals and experiments are performed. Eventually, it becomes time for me to present the piece of work I have prepared.

At the appointed time around thirty people stand surrounding me. Some of the most adventurous and creative people alive in the world today. Such big personalities all concentrated in one room. As they wait expectantly for me to begin to tell them a story…

*'One describes a tale best by telling the tale. You see? The way one describes a story, to oneself or to the world, is by telling the story. It is a balancing act and it is a dream. The more accurate the map, the more it resembles the territory. The most accurate map possible would be the territory, and thus would be perfectly accurate and perfectly useless. The tale is the map, which is the territory.*
*You must remember this.'* - Neil Gaiman – American Gods

Don't write anything down. Don't take notes…. Listen!

The following work is firmly rooted in the urban shamanic paradigm, I don't want its details recorded for posterity and 'set in stone'. I want the story of this ritual to alter over time, to grow and find it's own momentum. This is one of the lessons oral traditions teach us, if we have the ears to listen.

Our current concept of linear-time is limited in its malleability (bringing with it a concept of an enormous power outside of our selves, a concept we call Fate) and hence has fast become limited in its usefulness. We need to grow beyond this linear model and begin to work with different concepts of time, which can be manipulated with our Imagination and Will. If we do not, we will forever be limited by our own belief of the past causing the present, which in turn causes the future, and in this process we have no influence.

The terms past, present and future are used below simply for the sake of clarity. The divisions of past, present and future do not really exist. I like to imagine them as the Three Norns in Norse Mythology, three beings living together in the same place, at the same time. Just as stories in our heads exist together in the same person.

Let's for a moment consider the past. What we choose to call 'the past' is actually a collection of things we call 'memories'. All memories consist of is information received through the filters of our five senses combined with a good dose of imagination. As the memories dim in the conscious mind, the imagination fills in the gaps. This is especially evident if we tell and re-tell a story of something that happened to us in the past. Like Chinese whispers inside our own mind, the story changes in the telling as we embellish and expand certain aspects of it, whilst gradually forgetting other less important features. Our memory, and hence our past, is therefore simply a collection of stories we choose to tell about ourselves.

As such the past is perfectly malleable in accordance with our will and imagination as we choose to believe the stories we create. The only conflict arises when someone else has a different story to tell surrounding the same events. I would suggest that in this situation neither story is untrue. The truth is purely subjective, as psychological tests on witnesses to automobile accidents have shown. In certain cases the witnesses could not even agree on the colour of the cars involved, never mind the incidents surrounding the impact! What we call 'the truth' in such cases is actually a general consensus of the belief of those involved. Is 'a general consensus of belief' equal to 'the truth'?

'The future' is a concept similarly centred on belief. Whether it's a future state we desire for ourselves or a future state somebody else believes will happen. This can be demonstrated in something as mundane as picking up a coffee cup. I have to imagine myself leaning over the table, reaching out and picking it up before I can do it. This thought may occur a fraction of a second before I do it, but it happens. When we talk about the future, we tell the audience (be that other people or ourselves) a story, using the information gathered through our senses and a good dose of imagination (sound familiar?). This makes the future perfectly malleable in our own head. In telling the story we are creating a map for the future.

'The present', is this moment, Now! A fleeting, imperceptibly fast, experience. The start of this sentence is already a memory. The present is the only thing, which cannot be changed. The present is the experience of the story. It's a gift, and experience is the reason we create the stories in the first place.

The work we are about to do centres around an invocation of our core 'Magical Self', and uses this as a basis to evoke a utopian future for us to inhabit. Through my investigation into storytelling I came across a therapist called Pat Williams.. She wrote to several prominent successful individuals and asked a simple question: 'Is there a story which has influenced your life?'. In almost all cases the answer was 'Yes'. The individuals in question had not realised the huge influence the particular story they had chosen exerted on their life, until they pondered the question. This opened a floodgate in which they could see the story playing itself out throughout their lives, as a driving force and guiding influence up until the present.

If we enter the story which has influenced our lives in this way, if we invoke and become our favourite influencing character in that story. Then, being magicians, existing in the present, we would be invoking our Magical Self through the metaphor of this story. The driving force of our lives to this present moment. From this standpoint of the Magical Self, all the worlds of the past, present and future are laid before us… and anything becomes possible. We can even create a future world we truly desire.

'It is our will to create a utopian future for ourselves. Its birthday is midwinter 2012'.

I want you to think of a story, or a book, or a film that has haunted and disturbed you in the past. It usually first appears around the teenage years. It was a story that really made you think 'Fantastic! That story changed my life'.

As I start to think of my story, my limbs begin to shake. I am stood shivering to keep myself warm, it is unbearably cold. The people around me feel it too, as they all start to shake. I start to breathe hard and fast. My whole body, legs, arms and head are now vibrating in time to an hypnotic, fast rhythm. The music makes the breathing comes in waves of tempo. Periods of fast panting followed by periods of long, deep, fast in breaths and relaxed out breaths. The panting calms down the shivering, but then a fire rises in my spine. From my arse to my head, causing spasms and jerks to my limbs. The tempo of the music increases faster and faster, until you can't take it anymore, then it slows. Only to build yet again. Gaining in volume it feels as if a raging madness has taken over my body. Yet I must focus my attention on something. The story, my favourite story. I step inside it, right into the shoes of my favourite character. I become that character. I feel how that character feels. I see what they see. I hear the sounds and conversations they hear, taste and smell the things they do in my favourite story. I cannot stop shaking and breathing with the music as it reverberates through my frame.

The music stops.
I fall to the floor.

I relax. My head afloat, I let my breathing become shallower and shallower. I ignore my in-breath, it works effortlessly by itself, and concentrate on breathing out. I keep concentrating on breathing out. (Pause). I begin to feel my extremities getting numb, as if the room was below freezing temperature. I am cold. It begins as a tingling sensation in my feet and fingers, which disappears leaving my extremities empty and covered in ice. This icy feeling gradually works its way up my legs and arms. I concentrate on breathing out, everything is going to be OK. (Pause). As the ice creeps up my torso, it leaves nothing behind. (Pause). My body is disappearing. I concentrate on breathing out. (Pause). When the ice reaches the top of my head I look down and see my body below me covered in ice.

Feel the calm centre, observing my lifeless form on a wooden floor frozen to death in a sweltering August heatwave. I begin to see before me a hot summer's day. The dune grass hisses in the breeze, the waves climbing up the beach only to retreat to the sea once more. Cornwall can be beautiful in the summer, but the winters! The winters are cold and wet. The wind howls in the dunes, and the huge waves crash into the headland. The lighthouse drowning for several seconds as the water covers it. I see a house slightly inland has a light on. Midwinter 2012. Through the stormy rain, I see a beautiful modernist bungalow just in sight of the sea. Solar panels and turf roofs, balconies and decks. A wooden and glass studio amongst the cedars, completed and semi-completed artworks are seen inside. Vivid landscapes and portraits; magical pictures which capture the eye and entrance the heart. I turn, and gaze through the illuminated window of the house to see myself, Rach and Vanya throwing a party for friends and family. People are laughing, chatting, playing and flirting amongst themselves. Whatever they get up to everyone seems to be enjoying him or herself.

This is our house. Our garden. Our life. All bought and paid for with plenty of cash left in the bank, independent from any control but our own. People are friendly and new contacts, alliances and partnerships are seen to be made. I see two friends discussing how they met at our wedding. I overhear Rach, standing with our young child Eleanor and talking about her groundbreaking work in Art Therapy to a colleague. I see Vanya drinking with his college mates. I scan the room and see myself looking through the window at myself, looking through the window.

I smile, remembering the passage describing this scene in 'Now That's What I Call Chaos Magick Vol. II'. I turn my head back to focus my attention on my publisher. The books have been selling well, and I have people queuing up for artistic commissions. I take a deep breath, and feel how good life is. The storm will abate by tomorrow, and then there'll be waves to ride. The Sun might even make an appearance. Rach, Eleanor, Vanya and myself are fit, happy and healthy. We are financially secure, with everything paid for. We enjoy our lives. And are trying to help others enjoy theirs.

I finish chatting with my publisher, say my excuses then walk out onto the patio. The wind is howling, and the sea can be felt in the air all around. It's ozone clarity, and wild energy infusing everything. I breathe deep and let it scream through me. As I exhale long and loud. I look up to the window to see myself stood there, staring back at me in the storm.

I stare at the figure just emerged from the house, a silhouette against the bright illuminated doorway. The wind whips my face as my hand touches the glass. Smooth and cold as ice. I remember the cold and I remember my body. I feel my back arch. I gasp! And the in-breath is quick and fills out my lungs.

The Cold.
The Frost.
I remember my body.

I am lying on a floor, I am staring at the ceiling of a barn. Rafters span the inside of an A-Frame roof. I lie naked, and gaze into space for several minutes. Until I pull myself together, rub my face and sit up. Cold sweat dries on my body in the hot August air as I look at the bodies around me. Some people are still lying on the floor, eyes closed. Others are sat up and waiting patiently for the others to return. I remain silent until the last person is sitting up, then in true comic book style I exclaim, 'Bloody Hell! Where am I? What year is it?'.

That had been one hell of a journey!

## Growing Pains

It is a de-consecrated church in Southwark where we met, the other magicians and I. A huge empty space to be filled with our ideas, drama and laughter for a celebration at the pagan festival of Samhuinn (Halloween). A potent brew for inspiration and change at any time, but the company assembled are to create something this day that will have a profound effect on all our lives. Maybe it will be the invocation of the Holy Guardian Angel to be performed by us all spinning in two opposing concentric circles, followed by the invocation of Baphomet during a black mass using a willing human altar. I don't know what will cause it, but as evening closes in around the church walls, we process down to the crypt and willingly let something pass through our souls. I do not know it yet but this divine wind is to inform my future thinking on the development of Rachel, Vanya, and my magical child.

Soror You presided over the rite. She had been working with the demons Asmoday and Belial, and wanted to take this magical opportunity to be rid of them. The crypt is dark, the candles are lit and the circle and the triangle are drawn on the floor in salt. The seals of the demons are placed in the triangle as we huddle together in the circle. It is cold and damp, the warmth of our bodies does not even register. It gets colder as words are spoken over the seals. The smoke from the candles seems to coalesce into strange forms as it slowly rises to the low, cracked ceiling. The demons are there in the circle. I can see them as if the light plays behind my eyelids, but my eyes were open, wide open. Wide enough to see two Worlds at the same time!

The pact is made. The demons are allowed to play with us while the music plays, but then they are to leave us all and return to the place from whence they came. The music begins. A strange swirling tune, speaking of places in-between, where only the adventurous dare tread. Deep feelings rise inside me, emotions that flow from my eyes and nose. Here is no pain, but a sense of pressure, of something coming in from outside as if I was a balloon being squeezed. The pressure increases. More emotions flood out as the music's tempo and volume increase. And then ... Pop!

I am clear in my head and the music plays inside me. I do not see the demons anymore; but as others in the circle squirm and writhe, in pleasure and pain, I realise that the demons react to how you treat them emotionally. They reflected your emotional responses as a mirror reflects light. Approach them reasonably and calmly, and they will be reasonable and calm. They are here within you and without you, at the same time. This is the paradox. This is the key.

As the music slows I breathe calmer, and deeper. The clarity inside me stays, but as we laugh the demons back home, and burn their seals, I know I have gained some knowledge that will never go away. I have changed, the wind has blown and I know which direction I want to take our work with 'The Plan'. The Plan is a child, a creation with its own life force and energy. We did not simply create it by creating its glyph, it already existed and we had simply recognised it was there. The Child has a life of its own and we are merely its guides. The picture glyph Rachel, Vanya and I have created is the seal. We need to name our child, guide it and show it how beautiful its life can be.

To celebrate this realisation, the next day Rachel, Vanya and I each draw our child's glyph onto a piece of paper and tie them to the stem of a rocket firework. We walk in the evening light, at that magic hour when everything is thrown into sharp relief. We walk over the common across the road from my house in Buckinghamshire, and light the blue touch paper. As we stand together, watching the rocket jump into the great Prussian blue sky, we visualise the glyph framed by the evening's early stars. The rocket explodes with an enormous bang (my poor, suffering neighbours!), and the celebration is complete. We walk back in darkness, laughing with childlike joy all the way home.

## The Naming Ceremony

It is time for our child to have a name. And with the name comes form and substance. A naming is a very magical thing. We need to carry our babe in arms to the liminal font of the imagination. And we needed to do it together. This was not only my, or Rachel's child. It was our child, composed of our joint utopias. Which is where we sit now, on my sofa in Buckinghamshire, Rachel's beautiful face framed against its green velvet. We were thinking of Vanya staying for New Year at his Dad's. Hoping he was enjoying himself, and not getting into too much mischief.

It was almost time for us to retire to the temple. The candles were lit and the dark musk of the Abra-Melin incense filled our noses. We climbed the stairs hand in hand carrying a single candle to light our way. The rest of the house was cold, with the freezing temperatures of a New Year frost, but the temple… it was warm. It glowed with the light of a dozen candles, whose flames danced together on the walls as we crawled into the centre of the deep piled red rug of the circle. Our intention is to invoke our child in order to communicate with its being. We wish to clarify our wishes for it, and receive information as to how we could help those wishes come true in this reality. This is your naming ceremony.

Magical child, we are your parents and we shall have a fantastic life together. By the summer of 2002 we will have our own land and home, independent from control outside of ourselves. A home that is secure and warm, happy and cosy. A safe base, which overlooks the sea in Cornwall. A luxurious and spacious, self-sustainable dwelling from which we can explore and adventure. We will have all this, and even provide appropriate and convenient education for our children.

This in alignment with our higher selves.

Beautiful baby, if we have this by summer 2002, we will be able to immortalise your seal as a sculpture in our Cornish garden. We will have the time and money available to create it, in a relaxed and comfortable environment, yet this depends on the effort of us all. If you want to live in a world like this you must communicate to us how we can assist you get there.

We arrange the cushions and duvet to give maximum luxury and comfort. Then lie together, warm and alive. We touch and stroke each other's nakedness. Tracing patterns with our fingertips on each other. The skin of the whole body becoming more and more sensitive, as lighter and lighter touches are made to its surface. My body is tingling all over as I sit with Rach in my lap. Hardly a movement is made. I feel my hands lightly massaging the base of her spine and neck. I feel the two points connected by silver cord, as she does the same to me. We breathe together and relax.

Our lips almost touch as the breath is passed between our two mouths. A continuous roll, which sends me spinning. I need to concentrate on something visual, else the rhythm is lost. I open my eyes to gaze directly into Rach's. A third, unblinking hazel eye returns my stare, and I hold. We remain static, whilst the world sways in a steady circular rhythm. I sense a whirling energetic wind begin to rise up my spine. Gently at first, like the leaves blowing on a summer's day; but as the energy builds the wind gets stronger. The breath passes between us deep and quick. Odd Doppler effects happening as we sigh out, our muscles clenching as we breath in. The energy reaches the base of my skull as the wind feels like a hurricane. I keep concentrating on Rach's cat like eye, whilst clenching the muscles along my pelvic floor the throbbing becomes a pumping. I feel Rach come and this immediately sends me diving into her dark, central pupil.

We disappear into those comforting depths. I no longer know where my own skin ends and hers begins. We lose ourselves, as Rach's heat and energy becomes my own, in a blissful ecstasy.

Movement and shadows singing in the silence,
Light outside the window, presence in the triangle.

Love is the Law, Love under Will.

Colours in a pyramid, while the candles stood still and watched the Tiger Moths, because the children are the Guardians of the world. The Blue Planet light shining from its centre keeps on going, keeps on going. Like the Pied Piper's merry dance. I feel really good, calm...and relaxed. Everything is going to be amazing. The triangle sand appears like the waves on the shore, and it appears we are in a tent. And it is two years before this moment, we sit up in bed to see the avenue of trees stretch from where the side wall of our bender should be, and down to a world underneath...

Five spinning balls of blue light circle the pyramid half way up its sides, and an indescribable feeling of soft, clean sand. We sit opposite each other, gazing into each other's eyes. We are calm and balanced. The King and Queen in chess.

For our child we have a name. It is our child. It is 'The Plan'. It is our baby <u>Thep-Lan</u>! Hoorah!

That night the most amazing thing happened. A yellow submarine rose from the depths in the centre of Bristol. Right where The Galleries shopping centre is.

And at the same time Rach went to the scary Fight Club. It's in a dark cellar with big people. Rach knew why she was there and she fought only once, her opponent beaten to the ground. After leaving the club, she promptly went to the fairy shop, which was all racked out like a supermarket. The woman on the checkout asks Rach for a token, which sends Rach scrabbling in her purse desperate to find it. She does, and realises she won it in the Fight Club. With it she buys an apple (which she promptly devours!), and then brings loads of fairy-shopping home.

She comes home, and we sit up in bed to discuss her adventure. She sees the adventure as a positive chain of events, which led her to eventual victory. She returned home safe and sound, with the spoils of victory to feed her family. In the coming months, if she's brave enough to fight it out, she feels that Thep-Lan can be achieved. We're going to pull it out of the bag, as it were.

Later I perform a divination to see if I can see how we should proceed, in light of the naming ceremony we performed the previous day. I decide to cast the runes, as they are dear to my heart and home. Like a good poem they allow room for interpretation.

We clear the lounge table of papers, books and associated clutter, have a gulp of coffee, then light a candle and bring out the bag of containing the rounds of oak I cut long ago.

Thurisaz (Thorn) at the present time indicates an adventure is happening. With that go all the challenges, discomforts and chaos that adventure brings. To see this through we must be adaptable in attitude and learning. A forcing out of 'The Comfort Zone' into something else.

Laguz (Sea) oversees this apparent situation. The symbol to me of love, empathy and flowing energy, and a sense of losing yourself. Yet Isa (Ice) underlies this, pointing towards frozen development. Love will be our reward, as long as we can be patient.

Something new has been born, as indicated by the Ing (Frey) rune. This indicates our child Thep-Lan is strong and healthy. The seed we have sown is ready to begin growing.

Beware! We are about to move into uncertain times. The Dagaz (nexus point) rune tells us the twilight zone is just around the corner. I don't know what's about to happen, but it's gonna be weird.

# The Wedding

I stare up at The Long Man of Wilmington. A curiously androgynous chalk figure cut into the South Downs twenty-five miles east of Brighton. The chalk outline, eyeless, appears to patiently gaze North across the low-lying Weald towards London. The rolling hills of the South Downs stretch in a line East and West, seeming as if they are enormous green waves about to break on the shore of the flat Weald below. This is a timeless and beautiful place, and that is the message the chalk figure is telling all who stand before it. This is a place out-of-time and the Long Man tells us of boundaries between territory, between spaces and between times.

Every time I stand at the figure's feet I am reminded of all the other times I have stood and looked at its simple beauty. It stands not holding two staves, but stands in a doorway literally cut into the hill. Its hands pressed against the doorjambs, barring the way to travellers and intruders. This is an ancient and magical doorway, cut by our ancestors, and leading to the World-Under-The-Hill in which live creatures and beasts only seen in dreams and nightmares. It is said that Shakespeare first performed A Midsummer Nights Dream here at the feet of the Long Man. Commissioned by the Lord Of

Dreams it was first played in the open, on the natural platform on which I am stood. The audience on that historic night included the immortal Lord and Lady from the World-Under-The-Hill, namely Oberon and Titania (after all the play is about them, so it seemed only fair they should see it first!). The trouble was that Puck had been invited too, which meant that things very quickly got out of hand, and after lots of bawdy, humorous and sprightly shenanigans all is set right, the correct people get married, and love abounds.

I am sat in the grass telling this story to Mark and his daughter Rowan. They listen patiently knowing it is helping me to calm feelings of worry, anxiety and fear. I am dressed in a long-coat of pearl and silver. Royal Blue fleurs-de-lis adorn it and the matching waistcoat. My tricorn hat lies on my thigh high black leather riding boots, and my unbleached woollen trousers are making me sweat. I look north, the Weald stretching below us to the horizon. The birds swoop and turn circles against a background of a clear-blue, cloudless sky. I should be enjoying this fantastic day, yet my mind is racing with the hundreds of things I must have forgotten to do, with stage fright at the very public ritual I am about to enter, and with the anxiety that it will all go horribly wrong. I am sat in the grass telling this story to Mark and his daughter Rowan. They listen patiently and sympathise with me. Mark tells me he would be nervous if it was his wedding and some of the guests taking part in the ceremony were late.

I look at the assembled throng who surrounds me. All are family and friends, all have been invited to our wedding, and all have come as the person they want to be. Over 80 people stand upon the green turf beneath the silent Long Man. I see a famous racing driver surrounded by several fairies, medieval courtiers and Superman having a chat with a group of black magicians, and Pan sharing some bread with the Roman Legionnaires. I glance to the centre of our circle and notice Puck and the Cyber-Fairy pointing up the Hill. I follow their pointed fingers above the Long Man and see the silhouettes of our missing guests. As if The Long Man Wendel has opened his doorway, they begin to descend towards our chosen place of ceremony. Hoorah!

My anxiety and fear abate a little. We all wave and shout encouragement to the missing guests, as they slip and slide down the hill towards us. With smiles and beaming grins the latecomers, fire-eaters and explorers eventually join our circle. Brief greetings and jokes are shared before Puck and the Cyber-

Fairy begin to give orders and organise people. Lines need to be learnt and props assembled. People need to know what to do in the marriage ceremony, and when they should speak. Magical ritual is a strange play, designed to provoke an emotional response in all the actors, as there is no audience. When trying to marshall a group of independent and relaxed individuals such as these, some experience at herding cats is advantageous. The Cyber Fairy leads Rachel and myself by the hand, out of the circle around the hill. The last we see of the circle is Puck getting his whip out, to correctly position some unruly fairies. The Cyber Fairy tells us not to be nervous, Rach and I have done all the preparation we can. It is time for us to spend a few precious moments thinking of our love for each other as she and Puck take over the responsibility for the ritual. We should cherish these moments as they are the last we will spend apart. After we have exchanged rings we will never be apart again. I shall always be a part of Rachel and she shall always be a part of me.

## How We Met

We sit beneath the eye of the sun and remember the night we met. Five years ago it seems like only yesterday. The Vale of the White Horse and a druid camp organised by Julie and Ivan. One of a regular series of camps arranged to coincide with the Celtic Fire Festivals people would arrive and either pitch tents around the central fire, or sleep in one of the three communal 'benders'. These benders were huge dome shaped tent structures covered with tarpaulin, and capable of seating 50 or 60 people inside. People would use them to chat, perform healing, sleep, eat, have sex, shelter from the rain, and when night fell the benders would be used to shelter storytellers, performers and magicians.

It was on one such night we met. Ivan had come into the Mega Bender earlier in the day and asked if anyone wanted to do a fire walk. With my usual bravado I immediately volunteered, along with Rachel and nine other people. I had not spoken to Rachel very much, I was far too nervous. We had spent the whole day gathering wood and peeling back turf in the lower field, to reveal a trench about 3 feet wide and 15 feet long. In the centre of this trench we had built a conical fire consisting of all the gathered wood. We stayed together in our group of 11 members, watching the flames consume the wood and following the sparks rising into the evening sky. The heat was fierce, and the thought of walking in it seemed impossible! We each ground our chattering minds to a standstill, allowing the stillness and peace of the night to enter into us.

My mind is led down hidden pathways, overgrown with thorns, they twist and turn as my mind descends into a dark place inside me. A doorway in the cold blackness is opened and I see all my fears shambling towards me. One after another they appear to me as beings grotesque and deformed. I stand transfixed, unable to turn in that inky darkness, as if my head is clamped in place. I can move only my eyes from side to side, desperately failing to not see the demons placed in front of me. They smell of dripping pork and move forwards as if they are rewinding on a T.V. screen. They are seen moving in the stark white of a faulty fluorescent tube overhead. It keeps randomly flicking on and off, illuminating the disgusting scenes before me as if in an old black and white silent movie.

As the deformities approach, they begin to coalesce into one impossible freak of evolution. A parody of human form, its head displaced and legs withered to stalks. A straitjacket surrounds its torso keeping wild flailing arms in place. Blood and raw flesh hang between its naked legs. Yet the horror, the horror, the horror of this vision is not in any of this. The horror is that when the broken neck twists itself agonisingly toward me, it is my face I look upon. My face smeared in its own faeces, broken spectacles surrounding wide tortured eyes. This is my fear. This is my fear of my own insanity. Knowing that I cannot communicate my visions properly to the outside world for fear of recrimination, but unable to stop them entering my own head. There the visions remain trapped, seeking for a way to break out into the World.

I remain unable to move as the gibbering head violently sways from side to side, the eyes of the monster fixed on mine. 'I want to be you, or else I will kill you', it says. I have no argument as no words can escape my constricted throat. Its stick legs shakily move it closer with terrible, slow inevitability. The sound of bone scraping against bone and the sticky, sickly sweet smell of rotten blood fills my nostrils. It touches my arm with splinted fingers. Ignoring the boundaries of flesh it pushes in. I finally scream in horror and agony as I let it enter me. It pushes and squirms like an eel, fitting its hideous body into my own. A giant maggot burrowing under your skin, translucent and fat. My screams seem to last for hours, but I cannot stop. I have to escape the penetration of this creature as it pushes further and further in.

I grasp a memory of calm and peace. I am sat inside 'The Library'. Red walls lined from floor to ceiling with books. A fire is roaring in the grate, and the room is lit with a warm orange glow. Pictures line the walls, and the heavy wooden shutters on the windows protect me from the darkness outside. I am hidden in the safe room within my mind. Outside I can hear the sounds of the night. Howls, and screams in the dark. Body and soul being torn apart, by the demons of the night. I concentrate on the fire in the grate, the warming protector, the hearth fire burning to keep us safe and sound.

I look up from my reverie through tears to see the trench of fire in front of me. My mind is raging with nerves. A whirlpool sucking me down into the abyss. I can't go through with this! Walking on fire is not possible! I am going to be hospitalised! I have lost my mind, and cannot tell the others in the group how I feel. I cannot communicate properly, my tongue is stuck in my throat. I cannot breathe. I must be dying. Little orange and red fire-devils spiral up between the black coals and I have to put my hand over my face to prevent my eyebrows singeing. With the others I get up and begin to circle the Fire-Pit widdershins. My legs are not working properly. They must have gone to sleep as I sat down on the floor. Pain shoots up from my ankles with each step. The agony of walking is overtaken by my fear of the Fire-Pit. I don't want to do this, why should I?

Keep thinking of the sea in November.
Don't think of the fire!
Cold and wet November seas.
Don't think of the fire!

The fire. I remember a fire in a Library inside my head. A calm, steady, unquenchable hearths fire. I can feel its warmth on my face. Thinking of that fire brings warmth to my heart. A quiet moment in which to breathe. I find myself at the head of the Fire-Pit, and turn to face its length. Like an airport runway it stretches to the distance, glowing black and red. Sat in my favourite armchair in front of the fire in the library, I start to walk towards the far end of the trench.

'I have no fear. Fear is the mind killer. Fear is the little death, which brings total obliteration. I will face my Fear. I will allow it to pass over me and through me, and when it has passed I will turn the inner eye to see its path. There will be nothing. Only I will remain.'

As I repeat the mantra to myself it is as if I am walking down a gravel driveway. The stones can be felt pushing against the soles of my feet.

'I have no fear. Fear is the mind killer. Fear is the little death, which brings total obliteration. I will face my Fear. I will allow it to pass over me and through me, and when it has passed I will turn the inner eye to see its path. There will be nothing. Only I will remain.'

As I repeat the mantra I feel a tremendous rush of energy from the ground beneath my feet. A hot desert wind rising all around and through me, burning everything in its path. The heat is uncontrollable and cannot be contained. I must find a way to release it, I must give in to it. I must let the fire do its work in me.

I open the shutters inside The Library and see the flame wind rushing up past the windows. Nothing shall remain. The demons are evaporated in the flames, all their flesh and bone is gone. Their pain is ended, their energy sucked back into the Void from which they arose. Destruction and death are stripped bare before the divine wind outside. The demon took a hold on my body. It became me and by doing so it sealed its own fate. The stripping away of tortured flesh is an apocalypse of the soul. An Armageddon which leaves no prisoners. Inside the Library, by the hearth fire, I am safe and I wait for the fire to die down.

My feet reach the end of the trench. The all-consuming fire is gone. I jump in the cool, springy grass and shout with abandon and joy. I check my feet for the third degree burns I know must be there, but there is nothing. Only I remain.

The fire has burned away all that I was, leaving the pure core intact. The calm centre that retreated to the Library is what I am. The Greg is dead! Long live The Greg!

We continue to circle the trench until everyone has walked on fire at least once. A palpable feeling of magic is in the air, people have died and been reborn. We all feel alive, absolutely alive and free. We feel as if we can do anything. We are invincible! We are all Superman and Wonder Woman. As we all hug and congratulate each other, I walk up to Rachel and say words I never would have had the courage to before. I meet her eyes and say, 'I will probably not have the opportunity to say this again, but you are the most beautiful person I have ever met'. Tears fill her eyes and she wraps her arms around me, surrounding me in a warm perfumed darkness.

We sit beneath the eye of the sun and remember the night we met. Five years ago it seems like only yesterday. Rachel's eyes fill with tears and she wraps her arms around me, surrounding me in the warm perfumed darkness of her purple and green wedding dress. As we embrace I look over Rachel's shoulder to see the Cyber-Fairy walking towards us along the path. Our time has come. It is time for our Wedding Ceremony.

My heart begins to race, the nerves are kicking in. The enormity of each step sounds like the tolling of a huge bell in my mind. The tri-corn hat on my head shields the Mid-day sun from my eyes, and the ground underfoot is a carpet of lush green. I stand in the circle of guests. Sixty people, or so, encircle Rachel, Puck, The Cyber-Fairy and myself. We all stand at Wendel's feet. I can think of nothing as I stare in wonder at the scene before me. The people around us become Rachel's and my combined history. A distillation of our lives before this moment. All the guests are looking on with the power to end the dream at any time. My concentration in the moment is complete. All thoughts of past and future disappear in a rush. As if the airlock in my head which holds back the dazzling vertigo of the vacuum filled abyss, is opened.

As I speak, I. slowly. Spin. Clockwise. Looking. At. Each. Guest. In. Turn. In each face is the urge to continue. Nobody wants this to end prematurely, they all want the wedding to go ahead. A circle of flower petals issues from my fingertips, over the heads of the guests to settle in a ring behind them. A 'Temporary Love Zone' is cast. Hat held between the fingers of my right hand, the arms outstretched in a gesture of welcome and openness. The gesture of my invocation. The gesture of my calling to another. A calling to all that is free within the surrounding landscape and ourselves. A calling to great Wendel to open his door in the turf. Let the folk beneath the hill come forth and join in the celebration! The party is about to begin!

'Thank you all for managing to get here today. Today has arrived. Midsummer's Day. Our wedding day. To see all the people you love in one place at one time is a rare gift, and truly, truly overwhelming. Again I thank you all. Yet, do not think you are idle voyeurs to the spectacle before you. For it is said in Native American tradition, that it is lucky for a wolf to appear on your wedding day. Now, we couldn't get hold of a wolf in time for the wedding, so you all are to be the wolves for us. After a count of three I want you all, in your loudest voices, to howl like wolves. 1...2...3...Aaaaaaarrrrrooooooooooooooooooooooooooooohhhhhhhhhh!!!!'.

It breaks the ice. Family members look at each other as they half-heartedly join in. Looks of feigned embarrassment on their faces, checking to make sure they are not the only ones looking foolish. Once they realise everyone is howling their lungs out, it gives them permission to enjoy themselves and the howls reach up to the heavens, and down to the bowels of the Earth.

The fire-breather steps forward. Dressed in metal and furs, pale dreadlocks hanging down her back. Confidently she paces inside the circle of guests, fire roaring from her mouth in great balls of heat and flame at the four cardinal points of North, South, East and West. Gasps of astonishment from the crowd, as the fire breather flashes a smile and then the flames issue forth from between pursed lips. Blessing the crowd with heat and spectacle. Consecrating the assembly by burning away the outside world. This circle of grass is the real world; this circle of lovely people on the fairy mound is all that is real.

For the ceremony to continue we must know where we stand. Where this Love Bubble we are creating is placed in the landscape. Each one of the assembled company must find where they are. We all must find our own centre, lest we get caught up in the whirlwind.

To guide us all the preacher in the East turns outwards, raises his arms and calls forth the Hawk of Dawn. It screeches high in the sky as he welcomes its blessing into this circle. The Hawk is the Word and the Word is strange.

Then, in the South, the Taoist mystic turns to call upon the Fire Shakti's. His red and white stick held over his shaven head, he brings it down slowly as he intones the call, 'Raaaaaannnnn', thrice. When the Fire Shaktis on their Shiva beasts are seen on the hilltop, he stops. Their blessings are felt as they approach the circle.

Next, in the West the druid stands. She turns to call for the Salmon of Wisdom, which dwells within the sacred pools of the West. She calls for the blessing of water to be upon the whole company. As she speaks the words, impossibly it is as if water falls from the clear blue sky. It bathes our brows and clears our heads. We all calmly smile at the miracle presented to us. Nothing else needs be said, the experience is everything.

Finally, we all turn to The Horned One in the North, his antlers silhouetted against the sky. His legs are those of an animal, and his hooves stamp the ground as he turns to welcome the powers in the North. The Ancient Ones who dwell in the Earth need to be welcomed to the wedding celebration. We need the blessing of those who have gone before, lest we forget the lessons they learned well. The Horned One calls upon Gwynn Ap Nudd, and the Great Bear in the Starry Heavens; he asks them to bless us not only for this ceremony, but forever. May we love one another and make them proud.

Once the call to the quarters is made, Puck and The Cyber-Fairy stand close with Rachel and myself in the centre. The focus of the energies called, and the attention of all the beings (human and otherwise) assembled in a circle around. As we stand together, the calm centre of a whirlwind, Puck and The Cyber-Fairy recite a blessing they have made for the occasion.

As height calls to the deep
As the Earth calls to the Sun
As the Land calls to the rain
And the fire calls to the ice
As flesh calls to bone
And the heart calls to the mind
The lance calls to the grail.
So Greg and Rachel call to each other.

As they continued a strange sensation washes over me. I hold Rachel in my arms yet it is as if the bond between us is deepening. Silver and red chains are placed around us, holding us tight. Forcing us closer and closer to each other. Clothes touching clothes, skin pressing against skin, and still further.

As the Earth is bound to the Sun
As the tide is bound to the moon
As the ivy clings to the oak
As rivers merge with the sea
May the bonds of care and respect unite Greg and Rachel.

The chains are tightening, and forcing us closer still. Past the boundaries of our skin, the pressure increases and we are being pushed into each other. A public mind-meld, until one being standing at the centre of the circle. A being composed of both our bodies and minds, we stand there in rapture. We are naked in our ecstasy, our beings laid bare for all our family and friends to see. This is who we are. This is our wish for the future. We turn to the assembled company for their blessings, and see them in the joyful tears running down their cheeks.

As the space of a doorway
As the space between the poles of the Long man
As the space between trees in a wood
As the space between the stars
May the playful space of freedom always be between Rachel and Greg.

And I realise we are holding the ends of the chains. We were tightening them as they were wrapped around us. The bonds are as tight as we want them to be. We can release them whenever we want, creating a playful space of freedom between us. We hold the centre together for a moment. And then release. The chains are unwound and we are once again staring into each other's eyes. Only our lips meet, and then they too are parted.

We stand back and speak to the assembled throng. 'Today, in this place is love declared. Along our future journey together, there are certain qualities we would like to carry with us. There are some qualities we would like to bring in, to increase in our lives, and spread to others. These qualities are…

Joy
Honesty
Freedom
Companionship
Beauty
Trust
Compassion
Endurance
Passion
Dreams

May those qualities continue with us on our journey. So mote it be!

This is a reading from 'The Prophet' by Kahlil Gibran. In it he speaks of marriage.

'Then Almitra spoke again and said, And what of Marriage, master?
And he answered saying:
You were born together, and together you shall be for evermore.
You shall be together when the white wings of death scatter your days.
Aye, you shall be together even in the silent memory of God.
But let there be spaces in your togetherness.
And let the winds of the heavens dance between you.
Love one another, but make not a bond of love:
Let it rather be a moving sea between the shores of your souls.
Sing and dance together and be joyous, but let each one of you be alone.
Even as the strings of a lute are alone though they quiver with the same music.
Give your hearts, but not into each other's keeping.
For only the hand of Life can contain your hearts.
And stand together yet not too near together:
For the pillars of the temple stand apart,
And the oak tree and the cypress grow not in each other's shadow.'

We pause and turn to gaze at Wendel's Doorway, white etched into the side of the green hillside. The words sink in as if refreshing a desert long time dry. I see bleached bone against the sand, a dead tree lying in a dried up wadi. In the distance, through the doorway I see a tent, red, flapping in the desert breeze, which blows in an azure, cloudless sky. As I approach a figure dressed in black stands waiting. Blue in blue eyes flick up to meet my gaze and I peer into their depths. Blue in blue mirroring the cloudless sky. The cloudless sky of a Midsummer's Day above me, and I am back at my wedding. Looking up at the sky as red rose petals fall out of the sky.

Puck and the Cyber-Fairy circle Rachel and myself. They are calling through Wendel's Doorway to the Folk-Who-Live-Under-The-Hill. Calling to them to join us, calling for their blessings.

'Friends, we ask for the blessing of the Good Folk, The fair Folk, The Folk-Who-Live-Under-The-Hills, The Folk from our stories and our legends. The Wee People. The Sidhe. Those whom we must respect; who live here in this place. Who live here in this place now.'

The circling continues, as Puck and The Cyber-Fairy continue the invocation. The petals keep falling from the sky settling in our hair and on our shoulders. The same petals I cast outside the circle at the beginning of the ceremony are returning to us inside the circle. The fairies are bringing them back to us. Bless them.

'Can you feel them around us? Circling around us outside this circle and now coming in. Blessing these good people, these people who we all Love.
The blessing of Faerie.
The blessing of Elfin.
Each of us now get down and touch the Earth. Feel its heartbeat in this place. Wish your blessing and the blessing of the Fair Folk upon these people.
Blessing.
Blessing.
Blessing.'

As the words fade out of hearing I can hear a faint music on the wind. Flutes and bells on the edge of my hearing. Taking me back to a golden light breaking through corrugated iron on a Scottish Borders hillside. Another magical journey in a different time and place. The Fairie Folk, again coming to witness a change in direction. Giving it their blessing and watching over the proceedings. One day I will return, but until that time I will enjoy the duality of this time and place. Puck, the messenger between this world and the world of Consensus Reality speaks again.

'Thank you all. Now, take each other's hands. What a special day this has been. A special day in all our memories, a day none of us will ever forget.

'If we shadows have offended,
Think but this and all is mended,
That you have but slumber'd here,
While these visions did appear.
And this weak and idle theme,
No more yielding than a dream,
Gentles, do not reprehend:
If you pardon, we will mend.
And, as I am an honest Puck,
If we have unearned luck
Now to 'scape the serpent's tongue,
We will make amends ere long:
Else the Puck a liar call.
So, goodnight unto you all.
Give me your hands, if we be friends,
And Robin shall restore amends.'

It is done.'

People rush into the centre of the circle as if we are at the end of a football match. Cheers go up as the powers in the quarters are thanked and bid farewell. Wizz passes me a bottle of champagne to pop and hats are thrown in the air. As I ease the cork out of the bottle all goes into slow motion. The chaos magicians enter the circle and I realise what we have done. The ceremony was not only a wedding. It was the melding, and merging of Rachel and my spirits. All the people stood around us are representatives of spiritual paths we have followed. Christians, Druids, Buddhists, Agnostics, Atheists, Artists, Scientists, Academics, PartyGoers and finally Magicians.

As the cork flies out of the bottle like a bullet from a gun. The guests mingle and chat. In that one moment however they all raise their voices in a cheer, which splits the heavens. A cheer, which reverberates around the World, from Matt in Guatemala and Gina in Australia, this is a single cry raised in grief for the old and dead. A united voice raised in a triumphant cheer for what is beginning.

I realise this is the climax of all that has gone before. Now, we must look to the future and create something together that we can all enjoy.

A new journey.

The beginning of a journey called Thep-Lan.

How Does The Young Bird First Fly From The Nest?

And so we return to the 16th January 2002. And I have just committed the most beautiful of sacred rites. Feeling like God I took the body of my child, the paper on which Thep-Lans seal was written, and set it free.

I sit in the temple space, high in the clouds at the house in Coleshill. Thep-Lans seal sits in front of me framed by the holly on the altar in the South. I gaze at it wondering what to do. Since the wedding we have cared for the child. Thep-Lan has grown with our attention, and become more like us with each magickal rite. How long do you keep a child in your house, under your wing? How long do you shield and protect it from the outside world and its own experiences?

I listen to Mogwai penetrating my body and repeat the same question over and over and over…

'Who am I?'

I get lost in the music and it takes me away from here to a place of rushing wind. Images too fast and furious to recall speed through my mind, and its energy fills my body until it cannot keep still. Spasms and shakes rip through me uncontrollably. Too much… too much… 'She cannae tek it, Captain!' …

I must find a calm centre to this whirlwind, I must concentrate on something, anything. My claws scrabble forward and find a piece of parchment on which is drawn a rocket shooting out from grasping waves. I see it burning onto my retina, and hear its name in my mind.

Thep-Lan.

The demon appears amongst the roaring wind and flame. Hands spread as claws tearing at the carpet, trying to release this energy inside me. I bare my teeth and roar… it's all too much to think. Far easier to let the wind and flame take you away to that other place. My erection grows as the flames increase and the wind blows all thoughts away. I must release the tension in my penis. I roll around on the floor, moaning and losing myself in fantasies of warm flesh all around me. Pressing against me, penetrating every orifice in a beautiful ecstasy. The flesh enters me and I lose myself in bliss, saliva and sweat mingle on the paper as my body tenses. And still it continues, taking me higher and higher until there is no coming down. I am losing my mind. I. Am. Losing. My. Mind.

My body ov luv comes into its own I no longer know or care what iz real I only know what I feel and even that iz not my own it takes me and I luv it so much I cannot tell what is me or it anymore I feel only feel as my cock grows too enormous to be believable and squirts all over the paper on my chest and I lie there until there is nothing but black light. Light. A light in the blackness, and I realise I am coming out of it. A name, a name I keep repeating to myself.

I begin to say the name under my breath, louder it gets, and longer. I chant its name long and loud.

Theppp-Laaaaaaaaannnn.

Again and again I repeat the mantra as I lay on my back and see its symbol before me. The rocket shooting from the waves. The waves are big and dangerous, yet they are the powerhouse providing energy for the rocket to go faster and faster. The waves are the energy Rachel and I have created, and the rocket is our desire. It is all Thep-Lan, the demon child we have created, and it is powerful. More powerful than even I could imagine. It is threatening to be bigger than even us, and soon it will control our actions and life because its life force is so closely bound up with our own.

My hands clasped together in front of my eyes and held straight out. Pointing at the symbol glowing in metallic pink before me. A calm point is reached as I concentrate on the symbol. The energy overcoming my mind is flowing from beyond, through my belly, up my spine and down my arms. Like a liquid fire running through empty corridors and out my fingertips to the symbol glowing before me. As the fire runs into it, the symbol of Thep-Lan glows bright and the power it gains is enormous.

I realise I am the channel for the fire and it is leaving me untouched. I have become the calm at the centre of the storm. Watching from a distance the symbol of Thep-Lan grow and pulse with its own life. The amount of energy I can give my child depends on how long I can hold the centre of the hurricane. If I fall into the music then the centre cannot hold, and the power will be lost.

Like a stone touching the water as it skims across a pond, I find the centre of the wind and flames. The stone flying through the air is a falling into the music, but eventually I arrive at equilibrium.

It is now dark outside, and time seems to have been compressed. God bless Fotamecus.
I sit by the fire and consider my next move for the rest of the night.

Where did the idea for Thep-Lan come from all those years ago?
Where do any of our ideas come from?
From beyond our knowing. They just appear in the Realm of the Imagination. In this Realm we toy and play with them for as long as it pleases us, then we try to manifest them in this everyday world we call Consensus Reality. That's what we as magicians do. We find ideas and make them real. All the spells and tricks in all the books are techniques to help you to do this and you can pick and choose any that suit you.

This Is The End, Beautiful Friend, The End

I loved Thep-Lan with my whole heart and soul. We cling to those things we love, fearing that they will leave, or be taken away, and never return; but in doing so we create a prison for them, and ourselves. In truth the things we love so tightly end up being our gaolers. If we do not set them free they can never change and grow in their own time, with their own guidance. They can never create for themselves, only copy their teachers. They can never have their own life, and are doomed to repeat our mistakes. We have a duty to help them break free from this cycle and create new ways to live. I do not agree that this separation has to be a painful or difficult process. If approached with love, empathy and understanding every child can be guided to their own freedom. To support a child with a different worldview from your own can be very interesting. This is the point where you can teach, and learn from each other.

As a final act we must burn the glyph of the old Thep-Lan. Burn his body to set him free.

I return to the Temple and stare out of the window, over the West Wood and into the clear night sky. I salute the stars and say a prayer to Earendil as I hold the body of my child aloft.

And with that I lit the parchment on which the seal was drawn and watched the sparks fly into the great, black sky. Thep-Lan's body was burnt and taken into Earendil's keeping.

And so ends this tale of tragedy, indecision and adventure. So, dear readers judge me if you dare. For in truth the tale is never ended and you cannot really harm me, because if Thep-Lan never returns to us, then I will punish myself far more than you ever could. And if Thep-Lan does return I will be sat in Cornwall on cushions of red, feeling the salt breeze on my skin with my lovely family around me. So, I will not care about your judgment.

# Epilogue

We have a spring fed fresh water bath under the house. It is fed through pipes into the rough, regency built stone grotto whose murk houses the pool. The pool itself is about ten feet long by 6 feet wide and six feet deep. The water is icy cold even in this warm sunshine and lies like a sunken slab of pure black obsidian. The pool looks as if it is bottomless from the dark stone that encloses the water. A portal to an unknown world left abandoned from the set of a sci-fi movie, a portal to a cold vacuum of a world where there exists no life. To enter the waters is a numbing descent into death.

It was my turn to go in. I had volunteered to go first just to get the thing over and done with. My body still tingling and sweat pouring from the shaking meditation we had just finished. I stripped off my clothes and stood on the glistening stone steps that disappeared into the dark. You leave this world as you came into it bare, alone and shivering. This I realise as my foot goes numb; and as I descend very, very slowly down the steps, the numbness rises up my legs. My fingers go below the surface and I realise I am dying very slowly from the extremities inward.

The shock begins to kick in when the knife blade of the waters surface reaches the base of my spine. My balls contract and my cock turns into a peanut (a very small peanut) before they too disappear under the ripples. I look down and I can still see my body and limbs in the water, but they are very far away. The longer I look at them the further into the depths they fall until they are distant, very distant.

I see my heart pounding not in my chest, but in my belly. I feel its rhythmic vibration stretching my belly, until that too disappears. Then my shoulders and chest gently and very, very slowly are given up to the darkness. It is as if my whole life-force were being pushed up to my head. My thoughts are racing out of control and my breathing is ragged. My body is shivering unstoppably, and I must control it. Slow down the thinking and concentrate on something else. Anything else. Must choose something important...Thep-Lan. That's what we came here for, remember Thep-Lan above anything else. Thep-Lan, Thep-Lan. Exalt in his form, his beauty and all he stands for. Remember him, that is the way through the veil.

The head is the last thing to die and something panics when the water line reaches my throat. My body starts to convulse and retch. I try to concentrate on Thep-Lan. Remember his glyph, his seal. One thought, one image. I see my life's breath exhaled as a fog in front of me. The last act we all perform is to exhale. This one is illuminated by the eye of the Sun, reflecting off the jet-black water. I have stopped shivering, everything is numb. Dead to me now, I picture Thep-Lan's glyph in the centre of Apollo's eye as my head disappears, gliding under the surface without so much as a ripple made.

Calm
Silencio.

I am floating in inky blackness. No feeling. No sound. Nothing. I do not breathe, but something still survives. When everything else is dead there is something which survives if we can hold onto it long enough.

'You have to love life and death with equal intensity', it says.

'Holy Guardian Angel?' I quizzically ask.

The voice reaches over and pulls Thep-Lans glyph into its own heart. They are one. Sat in front of me on a wooden stool my Holy Guardian Angel smiles.

Then my head breaks the surface. I howl with joy and smack my hands together splashing water everywhere. I do a funny little underwater run on the spot, and then haul myself out of the pool. I walk outside and remember what it is to be warm. The sun dries the water from my body as I lie in the grass, smoking a cigarette.

Then I notice it everywhere. It buzzes and chirrups, talks and runs, flies and crawls. It is vivid colours and goose bumps. It permeates everything with the drive for change, it creeps into your eyes, ears, nose and mouth. It burrows under your skin and gnaws at your bones. It is Life itself, and it is all so beautiful. The grasses a carpet of lime green deep-pile shag. The trees made of olive candy floss, all set against a cornflower blue sky. The place is alive with possibility, so many births and so many deaths all happening simultaneously.

Among the colours and sounds I get a feeling. A warmth in my belly which makes me smile. I lay there in the grass and I am visited. The visitor calmly and carefully places a new symbol inside my mind. A combination of the Holy Guardian Angel and Thep-Lan, it is a new beacon. A new satellite navigation point to head for on this exciting map we have made.

Where will it lead us now? This new, fully mature adult takes us once more into the unknown, guiding our family towards our desired goals. I contemplate its possible strange paths as I drive to our new home in Cornwall. There I am meeting our friend Shaun the joiner to discuss plans for building the studio in the garden. The boot of the car is full of red cushions.

# Act II: Theory

Story

How does a tale begin?
Well a good starting point would be with a confession.

I am a storyteller.

Storytellers traditionally dislike any sort of definition for 'Story'. They believe it limits what they can tell, and how they can tell it. I personally, however, prefer the broadest definition available. Every communication is a story of one kind or another. There is always a teller and a listener, the former transferring information to the latter. For individuals to be involved in this communication they must be the teller or the listener. In communication where the individual is both teller and listener different parts within our own minds are communicating (or telling stories).

Stories are fundamental to our existence as human beings. The human mind has an instinctive hunger for stories, seeking them out and passing them on to others. The world of story is one of pattern, metaphor and analogy, and we human beings are driven to seek the pattern of stories through this language of metaphor and analogy. We must seek the completion of the story; we must know how it ends.

More than this though, is the role story has played in our evolution. It is told that Cro Magnon man first discovered this language 30,000 years ago, by creating fantastic images of creatures no one had ever seen. These were not simply representational images on cave walls of animals the first humans saw in the natural world around them; but supernatural images of mythical creatures. A boars head on a man's body and a man's torso joined to that of a horse. These creatures show that man had learned to break away from the natural world, he had learned a mythology. This new learning coincided with a revolution in methods and patterns that enabled Cro Magnon man to survive and develop into human beings. His innocent competitors in this evolutionary race were the Neanderthals, and the evidence suggests the Neanderthals never developed the understanding of stories. They became extinct.

The world of story exists everywhere in our world. Our world is suffused with stories from the gossiping neighbours, to the advertising billboard. All is story. We tell them all the time to ourselves and others..

'What did you do today?'
'What are you doing in your holidays?'
'Do you remember the time…?'
Etc…etc.

In the 1980's the Department of Education commissioned a study into the effect stories have on the learning capabilities of young children. It found that if a six-year-old child were told more than four stories a day, the child would have a mental age of an eight-year-old. If more than four stories were told to an eight-year-old they would have a mental age of a nine-year-old. Conversely if a six-year-old was told no stories at all during the day, then they were found to have the mental age of a four-year-old. The telling of stories does not simply increase the child's vocabulary; they teach pattern and metaphor. These, then, are the raw materials that enable the child to build their own model of the world. The stories act as both map and signpost for the listener, being continually altered and updated as more information is received.

I find the idea that 'Story' influences the maps we create of the Universe fascinating, and I am growing to appreciate it the more I study Chaos Magick. This realisation that each one of us creates our own map for the way the world (and indeed the Universe) function is a central tenet to Chaos Magick. Everybody creates his or her own map of the Universe, but if you are consciously aware of the fact then you can select the map you want to follow. The Chaos Magician simply treats all beliefs as maps and signposts to amazing, exciting, terrifying and blissful faraway lands.

In Chaos Magick this method of selecting maps of the Universe is called the concept of belief shifting. This concept enables the Chaos Magician to enjoy the freedom of choosing any of the infinite beliefs/faiths/disciplines/methods/ religions/fla-vours/styles/dogma/ideas/sciences/philosophies available to the human mind, in order to achieve hir desire.

For myself, I choose to see <u>all beliefs as stories</u> somebody once told themselves about how the Universe functions. How can a story be wrong? It's only a story, for Gods sake!

| Therefore | belief | = | story |
| and, | communication of belief | = | storytelling. |

In my own words I choose to tell myself the story that all systems of belief are equally valid in the objective Universe. This particular story I call 'The Meta-belief', and it is a kind of overall story which includes all other stories about how the world works. It is the reference index for the maps, if you like analogies. Once a faraway land has been explored to our satisfaction we can return to the reference index to select another map.

The question for we magicians is not so much what to believe, but how long, and how deep do you believe in something?

And here we have a paradox. Magick seems to work better the more belief you invest in a particular idea, or map. However, the longer, and deeper you believe something is true, the less likely you are to return to the Meta-belief The longer, and deeper, you spend looking at the map in your hands you forget you are exploring, and begin to forget about the reference index. You begin to believe that the map you hold is the only map, and eventually you believe in the map so much…the map becomes the territory. You begin to believe the far away land is the only land, and think that it is the only land you can explore. You become lost. No longer choosing your own maps, you believe only those ideas that fit into your far away land. Rejecting any ideas that do not conform to the rules of your land, you brand them as evil.

# Art

## *Art noun.*

*1. The production of something beautiful; skill or ability in such work.*

I am interested in the borderlands between the realm of Magic and that of Art, where exploration of this liminal realm can access the best of both worlds and techniques of both can be used for mutual gain. To look at the terrain of this region allows me to compare the Artist and Magician within myself.

I believe that practitioners of both realms are basically emotional rather than logical, and both seek to enjoy the journey for its own sake rather than rely on some ultimate goal for satisfaction. The concept of Truth in both realms is purely subjective and temporary. The artist does not produce work for hope of salvation in his twilight years, nor does he do so purely for the hope of financial security (though it would be nice!). The artist, like the magician, produces work to affect change within himself, within others, and the world around him.

However, there are differences and the fundamental one is centred on meaning. In the Magical realm meaning is a precious thing, a pointer towards the whole, while in the Artistic realm meaning has become an impenetrable jumble of associations which the Artist seeks to cut away to reveal life in its pure essence. The Artist attempts to strip away any camouflage, to leave the work, and by inference the artist, naked before the viewer. Through this the Artist approaches truth of feeling, and finds that is the only way to achieve resonance with the world outside.

Both attempt in their journey to reach for something more than that which we were told we could do. They both believe the only goal to have is the hardest, furthest, most distant and most incredible goal. Now, both the Artist and the Magician realise this search may fail and become mundane or it could be completely predictable; but the reason they do it is because it might be divine. It could be amazing and incredible and both think it worth the risk involved to just hope that might happen.

Both have an inherent danger, and this is a danger of the ego. The more successful you are the more you really believe you are doing something fabulous that's touching people – and it really makes them feel really good about themselves. That's when the ego has this horrible feeding frenzy. You become self conscious that you created these fantastic works, and fill your self with your own importance. The less you realise the effect your work has the luckier you are, because the chances of it having a little bit of integrity are better. I think that's a good reason to stop projects when you become self-conscious.

Upon becoming self-conscious you have an opportunity to shut up! In those periods of silence you get gaps in which you can view yourself and how your work has changed you. Then, you see, it all becomes an effortless work of Art, your life becomes this one long Art Project. Only when you stop do you start to realise why, and how, and who, and where and so on. Through this process of recapitulation you find a voice again, something to say, and the life as Art Project has a new momentum.

All works of art are collaboration, as the artist does not work in isolation and is influenced by the world around him and the people in it. Therefore any artist that claims his work as his own is deluded. Instead of complaining about stolen ideas, he should celebrate the fact that he gets to bring them into the world on behalf of everyone else. When the Artist and the Magician work together towards a common goal they must incorporate their differences. The Artist uses his obsession and passion for the idea to push the work on through difficult stages, and the Magician must make those leaps of consciousness necessary to initiate new ideas and mutate old ones when the work becomes stagnant.

# Holy Guardian Angel

What is the Holy Guardian Angel?

Well, there is you, the combination of everything you are. Your physical body, your emotions, your memories and dreams, your relationships, your energy. You are everything you can imagine and think. This is you.

The Holy Guardian Angel is everything you are not. It is other.

It cannot be described, for if it could then it would be part of you. The search for it is therefore not the search for a specified goal, but a great search for other. It is the search for some kind of metaphysical experience and unity, bliss and joy.

As you grow and your knowledge increases; so the Holy Guardian Angel changes, leading you further along the path into the unknown.

The magician is aiming to establish a set of ideas and images that correspond with the nature of his genius, and at the same time receive inspiration from that source.

It is your purpose in existing. It is what you are here for, it is why you chose to incarnate at this time, in this place. Its goals become your goals, it cares about what you do and wants you to achieve them. To ally your desires with its desires is to enter into a divine communication, which if followed with necessary action, allows the Holy Guardian Angel to manifest in consensus reality.

It is beyond culture and represented by something divine. So let's live for that. Let's not stay earthbound with the mundane ways of doing things, let's reach for the stars. And through that reaching the divine may just pull us up to somewhere beyond the quagmire of this dualistic Universe.

The way to understand the Holy Guardian Angel is not through theory, but by direct experience. It's a path of exploration and adventure in which the 'Self' starts to become conscious of itself as just another construct through which consensus reality can be viewed. Your 'Self' will fight this every step of the way as it manifests in a complete overhaul of your existence. Be warned!

## The Path

The Path is your journey from cradle to grave. The story of your life. It is every decision you made and every action you took.

Is where you are now where you want to be tomorrow?, or in one month?, or one year?, or ten years?

If the answer is 'No' to any of those questions then you have not arrived at your destination yet. You are still travelling The Path. After reading the Practical exercise in Act III called 'The Path' you have a decision to make,

'Do you take the Red Pill, or the Blue Pill?'

The Red Pill: You can decide to continue to live your life as you have been doing. Allowing people to present to you The Path. The world around you will still decide which route you take, even though you still think you are making the decisions part of you will know you are not. This story contains a special knowledge, and after reading it, to continue on The Path in ignorance is to forget. And you will not be able to forget.

Or,

The Blue Pill: You choose to perform the exercises suggested in the text. You choose to reach for something beyond what you were told you could. Beyond all previous choices, towards a place you know to be right. The Path is the decision to search for what you really want. You become responsible for which routes to take. You gradually come to know where you are heading, and like a beacon it shines to you, drawing you on in its tractor beam.

In this section more than any other practical experience is paramount. You don't talk about your life, you just do it naturally. It's no big deal it's just who you are.

# Demons

*'Every idea of the week can be described, and labelled, separately from the first person to think about it as an entity on its own. I believe that every time we move, think, do and speak we're populating the universe further. That's where I go to try and pull things back down to find out how they changed while they were – wherever the unmentionable place is that these things happen – that there's a way to retrieve some of them and bring them back so that we can then re-mutate what's there in an inspiring and unexpected way'. – Genesis P. Orridge.*

One way to enter a world view where Demons exist (and it is by no means the only way, simply the best way I have found to understand them) is to believe that every-thing in existence has independent consciousness. This is not mere animism however, as the gift of independent life exists for the inner realms as well as Consensus Reality. All our emotional states, feelings and drives can be viewed as existing independently within us. Let me illustrate this view through the following example.

I have a Demon within me called 'Anger', who is gifted at driving me forward when I am drained and tired. When I am weary he whips me into action. His teeth are clenched and the muscles of his jaw are tight. He hates the injustices found in the world and spurs me on to root them out. He is quick to manifest, and takes over my body when he feels I am being threatened or abused. He is harsh and cruel, caring not for the feelings of those who stand in his way. He feels justified, and is proud of his actions. He suffers fools not at all and will spare them no time, seeing and understanding their motives not through the thick red mist that covers his eyes. He is ANGER. His skin is like dark brown leather and he raises his fists to the sky, eyes wide he puts his head back and screams.

Now, I could draw a picture of this Demon to get a view of how he looks by transferring the list of attributes above into a representational image. He already has a name (Anger), and we could do some automatic drawing (As in the Method section of the 'Art' Chapter) to produce a glyph for the Demon. If I decided to collate a book of various emotional states (Peace, Fear, Calm, Joy, Vengeance etc. etc.) in this way, then I would be producing my very own 'Grimoire' of personal Demons.

'As Above, So Below'

One of the interesting things when dealing with these entities is that we tend to approach them using the same techniques as we do when dealing with people in our everyday world of Consensus Reality. We can choose to categorise these entities (and the people we meet in consensus reality) as 'Good' or 'Evil', creating 'Angels' and 'Demons' respectively, but I find this polarity a very limiting view, as your approach to the two classes of being will be very different. It is too great a simplification to approach the 'Good Entities' as friends, and treat the 'Evil Entities' as enemies. As in everyday life things are rarely as clear cut. Let's take the example of Anger for instance. It would be easy to generalise and treat Anger as an enemy to be feared and fought, but there may come a time when I may call on Anger for help. Particularly if my life were threatened in some way and I needed to fight my way to safety. If I have been fighting Anger, and trying to destroy him, then why should he come to my aid when I call him in my hour of need? There is an old saying which reminds us all that 'We ignore our Demons at our peril' and so I find it far more useful to look at each entity through their own merits and deficits. Dealings with individuals should not be clouded by generalisations, so for this reason I will use a broad neutral term in this essay to describe all such beings. Angels, demons, servitors, familiars and spirits will be called entities.

The work with entities is an important one as it forces you to evaluate how you conduct yourself in interactions with the everyday world. In my experience entities react to the way you approach them much as people would. If you work with the Goetia (or any old Grimoire) the people you are dealing with can lie, cheat, have huge disfigured bodies and more than the normal number of appendages; but I find the best way to react to these situations is if you were presented with them in Consensus Reality. How would you deal with a liar or a cheat normally? Does people's appearance matter to you? And can you face the fact that these entities exist inside, as well as outside, your mind?

As with people in Consensus Reality entities want power, independence and autonomy. This enables them to evolve and develop their own consciousness. They are like people without physical bodies and they achieve physical manifestation from the amount of 'libidinal energy' (See Appendix 3) you feed them. The problem is that the greater the autonomy these entities have, then the more able they become in achieving your desires. You want the entity to be independent enough to achieve your desire, but you don't want to give it too much power else you will find it in control of the situation very quickly.

A good example to illustrate this is a particular entity a friend of mine was working with. He had created this entity to act as a general good health spirit (called 'Health') that would cure him of any ailments he contracted. As soon as my friend had an illness he would perform a quick ritual, contact Health, and sure enough, within a few days whatever the illness was soon died out. The results were amazing. All went well for about six months, until my friend realised he was getting ill more often than he ever did before, Health was still doing its job, but my friend began to rely on it more and more. The more he relied on the entity to cure him the more energy he poured into it. I suggested he find out why he was getting ill more often, and after some work with different investigative spirits, he found out what was to blame. He had given so much energy and attention to Health that it had become very powerful. The entity had started manufacturing illnesses in my friend in order cure them and receive more and more attention. My friend learned this and immediately constructed a ritual in which he spoke to Health, negotiated a peace with it and broke off all ties to it.

Make no mistakes, in working with any entity, you are entering a power game and the entities understand that, even if you choose not to. Bearing this in mind, there are several strategies you can adopt when dealing with Demons, and if handled correctly they can yield some of the most miraculous results I have ever seen.

## Approach 1: Dominant

You communicate with the chosen entity as if it were scum. It will do as you say, or else you will hurt it. Be prepared to back up your threats with action. You will burn the seal of the entity if it does not do your bidding. You will destroy all evidence of it in Consensus Reality if it does not achieve your desire. You will tell all your magician friends that it is a liar and a cheat, not to be trusted as it cannot achieve anything, if it does not behave. You are the

Alpha male and the entity must do as you say to preserve the correct order of things in the Universe. It is not a real person, so you can treat it as badly as you like etc, etc.

This is an approach favoured by many old magical texts written by men who grew up in this territorial culture. It is a throwback to public school days, fagging and cold showers with matron. The strange thing is it does not yield very good results, as the entity will agree to do anything if you torture it enough, even if it is not up to the task specified. I choose not to approach entities like this because it takes up a lot of energy to keep in control and I would not want to live in a world where this is how people treated each other, but 'Hey! That's me'. Why don't you find out for yourself?

## Approach 2: Submissive

Supplicate yourself before the mighty entity, beg it to tell you the knowledge it has and in return it can feed on you. Politely ask it to perform your pifflingly insignificant favour once it has drained you of energy. Spend hours bowing to its seal, praying to it that it may help you. Beat your flesh with birch rods that it may feed on your pain. Bleed yourself that it may drink of your essence etc, etc.

I'm not going to go on about this too much as it invariably doesn't work as an approach without a lot of effort and not a lot of gain.

## Approach 3: Partnership

The classic deal with the Devil at the cross-roads. Summarised by the expression 'You scratch my back and I'll scratch yours'. Ask the entity to do your bidding, and you will give it something it wants when it has completed the task.

I find this approach works because you both stand on an equal footing. However it takes a lot of effort to maintain the even playing field. The entity needs to be chosen specifically for the goal you want it to achieve. You may be tempted to choose one from an existing grimoire, but if you do so new alliances are constantly needed to achieve desires. As well as this you have to keep your end of the bargain, or a whole heap of trouble can ensue. To use this approach successfully you must keep your wits about you, and be able to handle multiple tasks simultaneously. You are trying to keep everyone happy, including yourself, so the best way of approaching this is by creating your own entities.

## Sex

*'How can you learn to love anything, if you first do not learn how to love yourself'*

I like sex. From all the techniques of achieving gnosis, orgasm is the one I favour, because it satisfies so many of my criteria.. It leads to openness of heart, honesty, health and creativity through an expression of love (or 'Self Love'). I like sex, but this is no 'Lovers Guide' to satisfy your ungratified, consumerist desires. We are concerned here with the production of libidinal energy (See Appendix 3), for promotion of health, vitality and energy to direct towards desired goals. It is best explained through practical exercise, so I will present a series of techniques we used in Act I for you to enjoy. It is important to understand how this energy is produced and channelled within your own body, before you can successfully do so outside of it. Therefore the practical exercises linked to this section are concerned with 'Self Practice', alone and without a partner.

These exercises can be applied to both women and men, as human beings of any gender are equally capable of producing enormous quantities of libidinal energy through masturbation. This is perfectly normal and is effective in keeping the body and mind healthy and relaxed. If you feel ashamed of pleasuring yourself in the ways described I suggest you work slowly and at your own pace. The exercises will only work if you are relaxed and happy with your body and these new feelings.

Austin Osman Spare developed the idea of 'Self–love' and incorporated in it sexual practices. He apparently had a special tube of glass, into which he would place a piece of paper with the glyph drawn on it. He would masturbate with the tube and concentrate totally on the glyph at the point of orgasm. His sexual fluids would then anoint the paper and the energy would be transferred. This is a useful example to illustrate the practices of one particular magician, however, the essence of this technique and the useful part for this work is the generation and transference of libidinal energy through orgasm. The use of sexual fluids is not strictly necessary.

*'Your entire body is a giant electric machine: body chemistry (like all chemistry) is based on electrical bonds. It even runs on electricity. The energy you need to see these words comes from the egg you ate for breakfast; the egg got it's energy from the corn consumed by the hen; the corn extracted that energy directly from the electromagnetic light of the sun through photosynthesis' – K. C. Cole 'Discover Magazine, Feb. 1984*

The purpose of the magical operation set out in these pages is to generate libidinal energy, and then transmit that energy into a chosen glyph. The glyph then acts as a doorway, channelling energy to the entity associated with it. We are trying to give the entity enough energy to develop independent consciousness. I cannot stress this enough. If we are to succeed in this action we need to be perfectly clear about our intent.

The libidinal energy generated by the body can be directed towards any goal with the will and the imagination working together. It appears to be non-local in space and time (i.e. events / people / objects can be affected by it even if they do not occupy the same space or time as you when the energy is generated) and all pervasive. It exists in everything, through everything and between everything.

Theory associated with sexual practice is loaded with religious metaphor and jargon appropriate to the specific tantric belief system you choose to study. I recommend Taoist Tantric practice, as this seems to yield satisfactory results relatively quickly. Particularly anything to do with Mantak Chia, as he is sensible and practical. I strongly urge all serious students of Magick to explore a, or martial art that deals more fully with the methods of production, and channelling of, libidinal energy. (For this volume many of the techniques used can be found in 'The Multi-Orgasmic Couple' – See Bibliography at the end of the volume).

## Wedding
A wedding is a ritualised merging of two souls, a combining of bodies, minds and spirits. Two separate beings becoming one for a time to achieve a

particular goal or goals. The goals are traditionally criteria based, such as love and peace, but a partnership can be formed to achieve more worldly goals, such as achieving a successful business proposal. What separates a marriage from any other relationship is ritual intent. In business the ritual is a formal signing of contracts, in a traditional wedding it is the exchanging of rings. I firmly believe the ritual should be designed to provide a suitable context for the successful acts and desires of the people involved.

The next stage of our magickal adventure is to create a being to represent The Path upon which you are walking. One image which will galvanise your whole being towards a chosen destination. The destination should only consist of all the goals, emotional states and desires represented by the entities contained in your personal grimoire. If not you need to go back and think about what you really want. The method for doing this is by 'merging'. In a 'merging exercise' the libidinal energy of the entities are combined and fused. As they consist entirely (except for the glyph itself, which is burned) of libidinal energy, nothing is left of their individual selves. This merging is a 'Fourth Way' of dealing with entities, and avoids all the power games of the other three ways (Ie the Dominant, Submissive and Partnership approaches.)

One important consideration for this step (if you have not already thought about it) is who is going to come with you on this path. Who do you want to include in your new vision. This is important, as they will have their own Path that needs to be considered and integrated into this new entity being created. Do you have a spouse, partner or children that need to be considered. Do you want to involve friends and relatives?

Include any ideas, desires, wishes and criteria your loved ones may want to include if they are to have a say in the creation of this entity.

You do not necessarily need a partner to produce this libidinal energy in the body, but the 'Merging Exercise' described here does require one. (I recommend all Magicians try to work with a willing partner they can trust, not just from the point of view of trying out these exercises, but I think it will enrich your life generally!!). If a willing partner is not readily available, use your imagination to think of ways you can adapt the 'Merging Exercise' for solo use. I have done it simply by visualising a partner in front of me whilst staring into a mirror painted with the new design.

# Death

*'Even with all the advances of medical science, life is still 100% fatal'*

We don't like talking about Death in our culture because we don't know what lies on the other side of that black doorway. We tend to fear what we don't know, and we don't know Death. It is an experience of stepping through to the unknown, and it is a journey we <u>all</u> take at one point or another. Buddhist monks are encouraged to meditate by the Ganges where the bodies in their thousands are burned before the ashes are spread on those Holy Waters. Thousands upon thousands of bodies, and if you look upon them you cannot help but contemplate your own mortality, and the mortality of your loved ones. When you will die and be conscious no more; what that means to you and what you do with the rest of your time up to that point.

It is not for me as a magician to tell you what you should think, and believe, about this death state. I am just as in the dark about it as everyone else, and nobody knows what lies beyond this life. Nobody knows, but we can all choose to believe. All I can do is describe what it means to me within the context of this tale, and give you some practical advise with which to explore it on your own, in your own time, when you feel ready.

The glyph is the body of the entity and the doorway to have contact with it. The entity is not the glyph in the same way as you are not your body.

We don't know what is beyond the wall of death, we can only believe what is there.


*'I'm ready for the next big adventure because I'm weary of this one.'*
– My Grandma


Death is the final permanent merging of 'Self' and 'Other', of you and your Holy Guardian Angel. If you have the will and imagination to concentrate wholly on The Path at the time of Death, then the merging of your Holy Guardian Angel and The Path will happen automatically. This is highly desirable because if he entity created by this merging contains the same drives as your highest desires then its goals become your own. You have no fear in feeding it with as much energy as you can, because the more you feed it, the more your ideal world becomes manifest in your life and the entity is more than happy to help achieve your goals because it feels as if its own desires are being fulfilled. Everyone's a winner!!

The only problem you have is being able to return to your life, ensuring you can enjoy it with the knowledge you have gained.

For this magical operation the ritual 'death', or killing of the magical child described in Act I can be described as the re-integration of the entity (or idea) with the subconscious. The dissolution of the boundary once more between the original thought and the mind that created it. The merging of 'Self' and 'Other'. The whole process can be seen as an externalising of a particular idea, or concept, or desire, from the subconscious which is then consciously concentrated on and given greater importance than other ideas contained within the mind. When the idea becomes overwhelmingly obsessive it is reintegrated into the subconscious where it affects your life without you consciously having to think about it.

Well, that's the theory at least. Hopefully you, dear reader, are still interested enough in this topic to put the theory into practice, and brave enough to do some experimenting of your own.

Enjoy!

# Act III : Practicum

Question: Is the soldier responsible for the deaths of the people he, or she, kills during wartime?

Or, is it the sergeant, the officer, the general or the politician who gave the orders responsible for the deaths?

We are each responsible for the acts we do, the food, drink, drugs and information we place into our bodies and minds. Be aware of this when you are presented with the exercises in this section. If anything feels uncomfortable or makes you feel incongruent, then either change them until you feel good about them, or don't do them. For me Chaos Magick teaches its practitioners how to say 'No'. Non serviam.

## Story

How do we ensure the reference index is not forgotten and still retain the depth of belief that ensures the magick works?

The Chaos Magick answer to this paradox is that we should each find our own resolution for it. Outlined below are sets of exercises and guidelines for you to try out, and hopefully alter for your own amusement.

- Select a belief you find interesting. Preferably one you have no previous direct experience of. Then write a story beginning with the sentence…'I want to explore… {*insert name of belief here*}, and I will know I am ready to return to the reference index when….'

  (eg I want to believe in Zen Buddhism, and I will know I am ready to return to the reference when I have achieved satori, renounced all my possessions and am living on Mount Fuji etc, etc.)

Note: The essay can be as long or as short as you deem necessary, but you must be congruent (See Appendix 1) with the end result. If you do not receive a congruence signal for a particular piece of the essay then rewrite it until you do.

Note: You must be specific about when you intend to return to the meta-belief, or reference index. Make the point to return something you can easily recognise, else you may spend a lifetime exploring this one map! This acts as your safety net.

- Research the chosen belief system. Read all you can about it, talk to people involved with it, attend regular meetings, rituals,/ workshops, lectures about this belief and generally deepen your understanding of it. Create an area in your living space dedicated to the chosen belief and be sure to be aware of it every day.

- Feedback. Every week or two, put 5 minutes aside to compare your course in the chosen belief with your selection story. If you are off course can you correct it? If so, then continue until all your selection story criteria have been achieved. This is the point where fiction and reality become one. A most magical and celebratory time, so enjoy it! And if not, then you may want to explore another map.

Note: You should also pay great attention to the reactions of those you care about. If their reactions to your new beliefs are unwanted then you may want to alter your strategy until they exhibit behaviour that you want. This may entail looking at a different map that can lead to more desired results.

- Gnosis. To deepen your exploration of the chosen belief system, experience its trance states. These can be prayers/songs/rituals/drug use etc, etc, and may be performed in a social setting rather than a ritual one. Experience of these trance states (Or states of gnosis as the Chaos magicians say) can lead you more quickly towards your goal, as within this work they act as powerful indoctrination tools.

Note: An excellent résumé of various techniques to induce altered states of consciousness, and explanation of gnosis can be found in *Liber Null and Psychonaut'* by Peter J. Carroll.

# Results

The results you achieve from this work should be contained in your selection essay, and also be evident in your life.

If after several feedback sessions you are finding the goal unachievable, then simply return to the reference index and select another map. Again, be aware of the behaviour of those you care about as a 'Zen Master' turned to Satanism isn't going to keep his new found friends for long! Analysis of 'where I went wrong,' if your results are not good is incredibly valuable, and some sort of recapitulation exercise before you select your next map is advisable.

# Art

There is a part of you that knows what *beauty* is, or *Love*, or *happiness*, or *freedom*, or *honesty*, or *creativity*...etc...etc. It may be buried so far inside your mind that you cannot see, hear or feel it, but it is there. The problem is that it seems that part of you only speaks when you aren't listening to it. So you have to distract the conscious mind in order for it to be heard.

One technique to do this visually is to perform some sort of automatic drawing. Now don't get scared, we aren't going to be channelling the dead, or any of that. It's essentially a very simple technique, but you need to be loose and relaxed to let it happen.

What the following process creates is a magickal image where every element is deliberately built into the picture for its symbolic associations. We can work with this image in countless ways once it is created, but first we have to make it so.

Automatic Drawing
- Practice. Get some big pieces of paper and a pencil. Sit down and relax. Concentrate on slow deep breaths. Now, without taking your pencil off the paper draw lines of simple shapes across the paper. Try X's all on one line, then waves all across another, then squares, then triangles, then 's' shapes. Invent new shapes, but make sure they are repeated all across the page.

- Don't worry if you draw over previous lines, and don't worry if it doesn't look pretty. That's not the point. What is important is the freedom of movement and looseness of the hand and wrist. After you feel fully loosened up (usually 5–10 minutes) then we can start drawing.

- Sit quietly in front of your paper, close your eyes and think of a time you experienced something of *beauty*. Relax. Breathe deeply and place your pencil on the paper in front of you. As you re-experience this beautiful time, allow the images, sounds and feelings to enter your mind. Increase the size of the images, the volume of the sounds, and the intensity of the feeling. And as you do this allow your pencil to make marks on the paper. You do not need to take the pencil off the paper, simply allow it to glide across the paper's surface. Concentrate on experiencing the *beautiful* time, and allow yourself to enter it fully. As if you are there and as you do so keep the pencil in your relaxed hand drawing on the paper.

- When you feel ready to end this session you may lift the pencil from the paper. Open your eyes and turn your paper over so you are not tempted to look at it yet.

- Go and do something else, preferably something physical, or preparing food and drink.

- Now, after your break, come back to the image you have created during your session and study it. Are there any recognisable images in it? If so, then accentuate the lines that make those images (I usually go over them with ink) and make the images clearer. They can be as simple as a circle, or as complex as you can imagine. Play with them; see if you can make faces or animals, or geometric designs. Anything can come out and allow the images to emerge from the depths of the paper.

- When you have had enough, place the tracing paper over your images and trace them onto a new sheet of paper. Throw the old piece of paper away, or burn it!

- Look at your new piece of paper, and the images on it. Begin to combine and simplify them into one image. You may need to use several pieces of paper before the crystallisation process is complete, but remember to destroy the previous pieces of paper as you go.

- To end this process you should have one easily repeatable image that represents the whole experience you enjoyed. Not just the things you saw, but also the sounds and feelings you experienced. All sense impressions of that moment in time and anything linked to that time are all contained within your crystallised image. This crystallised image is called a glyph, and here we have created a glyph for *beauty*.

Note: This process can be repeated for any emotional state that has been experienced. However, if you cannot recall ever experiencing a particular state (*happiness*, for example), then simply *guess* what that state would be like, imagine what it would feel like, sound like or look like. The more you work with that feeling in this way, the more familiar you become with it, and the more you will recognise it in your life.

### The Holy Guardian Angel

Create time and space to perform this ritual on a daily basis, upon waking is preferable as the self discipline needed to do this helps your resolve on the days when you can't be bothered!! (And we all get days like that. Oh yes! We all get days like that!)

· Clear your mind of clutter by inducing a trance state of choice.

· Perform the automatic drawing exercise in the Art chapter above, but instead of remembering a time when you saw something of *beauty*, imagine what your *Holy Guardian Angel* could be like. Picture it, hear it and feel it. Feel free to change anything that doesn't seem to fit, and play with things like size of image, colours, volume, pitch, brightness, intensity, texture, and pressure until you feel congruent with your experience of your *Holy Guardian Angel*.

· Carry on with the automatic drawing exercise until you have created a glyph to represent your *Holy Guardian Angel*.

Note: It is *not* normally necessary to recreate the glyph every day. Once the *Holy Guardian Angel* glyph has been created, and you are happy with it keep using the same image until you feel it needs changing. At such times it is advisable to destroy the old image to avoid confusion of thought.

· Concentrate on the glyph you have created. How does it make you feel? Does it bring to mind an image or sound, or feeling? If so then increase the intensity of the experience, and if not then guess what images, sounds or feelings the glyph would produce if it could. Then increase their intensity.

- From these feelings, sounds and images try to imagine what your *Holy Guardian Angel* would look like if it were present in the room with you now. Would it have a smell, or a taste associated with it?

- Continue building this entity until you feel it is fully formed. Then you verbalise out loud your wishes and aspirations. This should be done spontaneously from the heart. Be honest and use any tone of voice you feel is appropriate, from humbling on your knees in prayer to shouting proclamations. Bear in mind that this is your genius, and you should treat it as such.

- Allow silent spaces in your verbalisation in order that the *Holy Guardian Angel* can communicate with you. After a while it may reveal images, names and spiritual principles by which you can assist its manifestation further.

- Return by concentrating on the glyph of the Holy Guardian Angel in silence for a brief period.

- Carry on your day as you will.

- At the end of the day before you sleep spend a couple minutes going over the events of the day. What went well and what didn't? What could you change to make tomorrow even better?


Warning: I know people who appear to have become spectacularly mad from continually doing this exercise. To avoid this you may want to put a strict time limit on the period of daily practice (i.e. one or two lunar months), and be very aware of the behaviour people you care about exhibit around you. If they seem to be acting weird, it is possible you are causing them to, so I seriously recommend having someone you can discuss your ideas with (i.e. a mentor, close friend or other people in a magickal group). This gives you another viewpoint and invaluable honest information on which you can take action if necessary.

# Results

The purpose of this invocation is to establish a set of images and ideas that correspond to your genius. It is recommended that these images, words and sense impressions be kept in a diary as soon as you can, otherwise they will be easily forgotten.

Feel free to use the automatic drawing exercise to crystallise anything that seems a bit fuzzy into a visual image, as we will need all these for future work.

## The Path

What I invite you to do is read the following story.

I hope you find it interesting and engaging. So sit back, turn off the telephone, get comfortable, and relax.

There was once a man called Edward Burnays who believed that people were essentially stupid, and because they were stupid they could be controlled. Before the First World War Burnays was a successful concert promoter in the U.S. representing the likes of opera singer Edward Carusso. He carried on happily in his chosen career until America joined the Great War, whereupon he was put on the payroll by the U.S. government to handle the media representation of the fighting in Europe. Burnays came up with the masterstroke of making people believe in a cause to such an extent that they were prepared to lay down their lives for it.

## Edward Burnays invented propaganda.

After the Great War, Burnays thought that if the techniques he had developed worked during wartime, they would work equally well in peacetime. He looked at where the power lay in peacetime, and began to represent the major oil and tobacco corporations. He noticed that smoking cigarettes was a distinctly male habit, and that smoking for women meant overcoming a social taboo. In 1920 there was a huge Fourth of July parade in New York. Burnays paid 20 or 30 female debutantes to march in the middle of the parade smoking cigarettes. Then he sent a release to all the major New York daily newspapers saying that a group of suffragettes were planning on hijacking the parade, and in their defiance of social restrictions imposed on them as women they were going to light cigarettes as 'torches of freedom'. This was a huge story at the time, perfectly timed to coincide with the general rise of female empowerment. Sales of cigarettes soared and Burnays' tobacco corporation clients never looked back.

Edward Burnays didn't sell things by appealing to the general public's practical need (i.e. how many miles to the gallon? how low is the maintenance? Is it healthy for my family or me?). He sold things by appealing to their emotional desires, and those desires could be manipulated.

## Edward Burnays invented lifestyle marketing.

In 1939 Edward Burnays was commissioned to produce the central exhibit in the World Trade Fair held in New Jersey. He created a vision of a utopian future with sleek, clean monorails, multiple lane highways and cheap convenient products for all. Everyone owned a car, and everyone travelled in aeroplanes. Fossil fuel power stations provided energy for everyone and major corporations had huge skyscrapers dedicated to them. The exhibit was a huge success for Burnays and no one was more pleased than his clients, the oil corporations whose names appeared on the tops of his model skyscrapers.

## Edward Burnays sold us the future, and we bought it.

And these are legacies we are still living with today. 80 years on we buy our cars because we want the rugged, fast, free and easy lifestyle that product represents. We still send our loved ones to die in wars because we are sold the belief we are fighting on the side of the 'Great and Good'. We have multiple lane highways, and cars and aeroplanes, and plastic products of every kind, but where do we take it from here?

To answer that question I would like to tell another tale. This one is about a storyteller and therapist called Pat Williams. Whilst studying and collecting stories from around the globe, Pat Williams. wrote to many of the people she could recognise as high achievers in their chosen fields. In the letter she asked each person a simple question.

'Was there a story that had once affected and haunted you in your life, and made a difference to what you did?'

Not only did she find that each person did indeed have a story, which had affected him or her, but that the stories directly paralleled the person's life. A famous deep-sea diver was greatly affected by the story *'Swallows and*

*Amazons'*, an explorer by *'Robinson Crusoe'* and a scientist by *'The Little Engine That Could'*.

Now, I invite you to find the story that affected you. Think back to see if you can find it in your memory. It could be a book, film, T.V. programme, radio broadcast, direct experience or a family tale. The medium isn't important, because we are looking for a story that made a difference to what you did. Take as long as you like to find this story before you continue reading, and don't worry if one doesn't spring to mind immediately. Good places to start are with your favourite book, or film, or TV series and examine characters or themes that appeal to you. People with more than one favourite story often find there is a common theme (or character) in them all, which strikes a chord.

Once you have discovered your story I ask you to find the character in it you most connected with. Which was your favourite character in that story. And, as you think of that character I ask you to experience the story through their eyes.

What would they see?

What would they hear?

What would it feel like?

And as you experience the story through your favourite characters eyes I ask that you play with the clarity of the images, the brightness of the colours, the volume of the sound, its pitch and resonance until they are as realistic as possible.

What clothes are you wearing?

How do they feel against your skin?

Are they rough or smooth?

What is the temperature like and to what extent can you feel it?

As you bask in the story I invite you to recognise how it has affected the decisions in your life, from first hearing it all that time ago…follow it…right up…to the decision…to read this book…where you are…

*now…*

…from this present moment… I would like you to use your imagination to travel with me into the future…I would like you to imagine an *ideal* future for yourself, and the world. Travel to your best guess at *Utopia*.

How will you know when this ideal future is here?

Where are you?

What can you see?

What sounds can you hear?

Feel the tangible things around you. What textures have they got?

How do people interact?

What do they use for fuel?

How do they travel around?

I ask that you describe the scenes before you, and record them in some way. Make them as detailed as you possibly can, concentrate on descriptions of things that interest you.

Write the story of your Utopia.

Write the story of your life.

And when you feel ready, you may return to your everyday consciousness, refreshed and invigorated. Ready to go out into the world and make your visions a reality.

# Results

As you write your Utopia and work with it, you do so in the knowledge you are free to change it any way you choose. You can work with it in so many ways, but I will outline a few below only as ideas to pick up, or discard as you see fit.

- Take interesting elements in your story and imagine the closest equivalent in this reality. What branch of the sciences, magic, religion or arts could contain more information about it? Research the interesting stuff you are writing about. Go to libraries, the Internet, lectures, workshops etc... (Does this sound familiar?) And meet people that are working in that area. Talk to them, get involved and see if your research can expand your Utopia and make it realistic.

- What 'criteria' (See Appendix 2) are important to your Utopian self, and the society of your ideal world? Make a list of phrases that describe them, perform the automatic drawing exercise on each of them. This should give you a batch of glyphs representing these values. Then work with them each in turn in the same way as you did when invoking your Holy Guardian Angel.

● Which people are close to you in your new Utopia? Are there friends and family involved, a partner or spouse? Do you want, or have, children? If so then the wishes of these people need to be taken into account. One way to integrate their desires would be to throw a party, and get each one of them to draw or paint something that represents their Utopia on a huge piece of paper. Then crystallise these images into a glyph as we did in the 'automatic drawing' exercise. (Alternatively they could read and perform the exercises in this book. 'Go on Grandma, you'll love it honestly!')

● Develop strategies to help bring your Utopia into existence. Who would you involve? How would you persuade people to give you help without them thinking you crazy?

● Produce works of art, music, textiles, or poetry that you can imagine existing in your Utopia. Or, design and produce everyday objects you write about in your Utopian story.

Whatever you do, *enjoy it*, it should be fun or else it's not worth doing in my humble opinion. If nothing else you will find more material to help pad out your story.

Happy Exploring!

## Demons

● Prepare the altar space with heavy, smoky incense, music and candles.

● Choose one of the glyphs from the 'criteria' exercises in the previous chapter and place it in, or near the incense.

● Do some vocal warm-up or singing exercises. A suggestion would be resonating vowel sounds and feeling where they vibrate within the body.

● Sit for a few moments, relax and clear your mind, then begin to concentrate on your breathing. In…out…in…. out…. in…. out….

in…. out…. In…. out…and as you focus on your breathing. in….
out…You gaze at the glyph…. in…out…. Begin to speak aloud the
name and attributes of this entity represented by the glyph…Let your
tongue run loose, uninhibited and free…. make sounds and noises the
entity likes and understands…establish a rapport with the entity…
In…Out…In… Out…. and continue to breathe….Relaxed and
aware….feel your concentration focused on the glyph….keep your
eyes open at all times….relaxed and aware….you can gaze into the
depths of the incense….hazy and small at first….In…Out…you see an
entity beginning to take shape….it grows in size and you notice its
colours….becoming sharper and more focused….the entity is talking to
you….In….Out….relax, and ask the entity if its name is the same as the
glyphs criteria….the voice you hear may be faint…and as you concentrate
on it….the voice becomes clearer and louder…

- Continue asking questions of the entity and communicate with it. You
  could ask it what it enjoys, or how it may help you achieve your specific
  goal. Ask what it wants, and discuss various topics with it. Don't limit
  your questioning to 'magickal matters', a good way of determining the
  entity's character is by reviewing your day with it. Ask the entity how it
  would have dealt with certain issues or situations that have arisen in your
  everyday life. Treat this as advice from a friend, not as an order from a
  superior intelligence.
- Record as much as you can from these communications. A Dictaphone
  may be useful, but certainly afterwards write down what is said.
- Create a 'personal grimoire' using your 'criteria' glyphs. Look at each
  of those entities and compile its glyph, name, attributes, physical
  appearance and personality. Include any communications you have had
  with that entity, and the approach used.
- Make sure you remain aware of your overall focus. Record any results
  you get as far as goals are concerned.
- I would suggest working with each entity in your 'personal grimoire' for
  at least one week, before you decide to move onto the next.

- With all the entities in your personal grimoire make sure you have a
  personal relationship you are happy with. Before you move on make
  sure you are familiar with them all.

Enjoy yourself, and good luck!

# Sex

It is necessary to practice and learn as much as you can about the following preliminary exercises before you go forward and put them together in the method described below. They seem difficult at first, but with regular practice they become easier.

### Breathing / Shaking

This exercise loosens the body, not only physically but also emotionally. It leaves the body relaxed and fluid, enabling you to move energy around your body more easily.

### Breathing

- Begin to breathe through your mouth. Inhale deep and fast through your mouth, *and relax your body when you exhale*. This is very important to avoid hyperventilation.
- Practice this breathing for a few minutes and then stop. Notice the feelings in your body. It is very physically demanding, but after a while your oxygen levels within your body rise and it becomes easier.

Important: If at any point you feel cramp, or stitch, then begin to pant as shallowly as you can, through your mouth. (As if you were a dog!!). Keep up this shallow breathing until you feel the cramp subside. Then resume with the deep, fast inhalations and relaxed slow exhalations.

### Shaking

E.g. breathe normally. Stand up and shake your hands and arms. Keep the wrists, elbows and shoulders relaxed and shake them as hard as you can. After a couple of minutes stop and feel the difference between the sensation in your arms and the rest of your body.

Does it feel warm, humming and tingly? It should, and this is the sensation we want to produce throughout the body. It becomes very physically demanding so *know your limits*!! If you need to increase your levels of fitness then gradually build up the amount of time you perform it.

- Lift one leg off the floor and shake your foot. Relax your ankle and rotate your knee, keeping it relaxed. After a couple of minutes try the other leg.

- Now place both feet on the floor and begin to vibrate your legs as if they are shivering. As you do this keep your body relaxed and begin to shake your hands and arms.

- Let your torso join in and begin to perform the deep breathing exercise outlined above.

- If you are tense in any part of your body, then vigorously shake it. If your legs get tense then lift each one off the floor, relax your ankle and shake it. Whilst doing this exercise remember to breathe, it's easy to forget.

- Continue for about 5–10 minutes. Then stop. Stand still and relax. Let your breathing return to normal and feel the sensations in your body.

## Multiple Orgasms For Men and Women

Contrary to popular belief, both men and women can achieve multiple orgasms. These are particularly useful in a magical context as the orgasm produces huge amounts of libidinal energy (see Appendix 3). This energy is released, and dispersed during ejaculation, but can be controlled and directed by utilising various techniques to hold back the ejaculation. These exercises also allow the practitioners to increase the build up of libidinal energy during sex. As the exercises are different for men and women to achieve this I will deal with them separately below.

### PC Muscles

However, the one most important exercise, which is common to both men and women, and is essential in achieving multiple orgasms for both, is the clenching of the muscles around the genitals, perineum and anus. These muscles are commonly called the PC (pubococcygeus), or 'pelvic floor' muscles. These muscles cause the rhythmic contractions in the pelvis and anus during orgasm and also regulate the flow of urine. Stronger PC muscles give stronger erections and ejaculatory control in men, and will increase the pleasure and ease of orgasm in women. So it's worth everyone's while trying to develop them!!

The simplest way to describe the feeling and explain how to exercise these PC muscles is by stopping and starting the flow of urine next time you go to the toilet. It may be sore, or sting at first as you are exercising a new muscle, but this should stop after a few weeks. If not then consult a doctor as you may have some sort of urinary infection and you should get this cleared up before continuing. If done correctly women should have the sensation that they are pulling their urethra and vaginal area up slightly into the body.

Note: Throughout these exercises breathe through the nose as this warms and filters the air. Breathe deeply using your belly and don't just use your chest. It is worth practising this for a few moments and the next time you go to the toilet try the following:

1. Inhale as you get ready to urinate
2. Exhale slowly, and forcefully push out the urine (clenching your teeth intensifies this)
3. Inhale and contract your PC muscle to stop the flow of urine mid-stream.
4. Exhale and urinate again.
5. Repeat until you are finished.

This exercise gets you used to the feelings associated with strengthening the PC muscles, and once you have tried it a few times begin to vary the exercise to clench 'dry' during your normal day. Try a few clenches when waiting for a bus, or whenever you're bored, if nothing else it is a good cure for boredom! You could try clenching the individual PC muscles (at the base of the penis in men (or urethra in women), perineum, outer anal ring and inner anal ring in turn, or you could practice clenching while inhaling. Once that is becoming second nature then try clenching whilst exhaling. Get used to clenching the PC muscles with different breath techniques and also try clenching and relaxing the muscles for various lengths of time (try 10 seconds clenched, then 10 seconds relaxed etc., etc.). Feel free to use your imagination and conjure up different exercises to keep your interest up.

## Storing energy in the navel

Before you learn how to draw energy up from your genitals into your head, it is important to learn how to bring it down into your navel area. This is because the Taoists believe the abdomen can safely store far more energy than the brain. The navel acts as this energy store and it enables the energy to be released slowly to the organs of the body at a later date when needed. The Indian tantrists believe the energy should be channelled from the genitals (and root chakra) to the brain, which can lead to very mind altering experiences, but the energy can have unexpected effects and so should not be stored there for too long. I recommend the Taoist method first as it is the safest and from my experience yields the best long term results.

● Start by relaxing. Breathe deeply and evenly using the belly.

● Touch your navel lightly with your fingertips and gently pull them apart as if opening the abdomen. Let your fingers come to rest on the belly about 10cm apart.

● Touch the tip of your tongue to the front roof of your mouth (There is an indentation on your palate about 1 – 2cm from the top of your front teeth). This indent connects two separate energy channels in your body (One channel goes up your back, and the other comes down your front), and your tongue in this position closes the circuit. It allows the energy from your brain to descend down your tongue and throat, through your chest to your abdomen.

● Smile as you focus your attention on your navel, allowing the corners of your mouth and eyes to soften. Feel the sun shining down on you and as you do so feel warm energy descend through your head and torso to your abdomen. Let the energy gather there and imagine it spiralling around your navel to help it absorb.

## Female multiple-orgasm practice

Now, I am no expert here, as far as female solo practice is concerned. So all I can do is illustrate the key points to achieving multiple orgasms for women. I strongly recommend all women to research this subject themselves and recommend any texts by Mantak Chia.

● Everyone can achieve multiple orgasms. Choose an appropriate date and suitable undisturbed length of time for orgasmic play/practice and ensure you keep to it!.

- Relax. Create a sensual atmosphere conducive to lovemaking. Use your imagination and any appropriate erotic films or literature to explore your fantasies. Many people find soft cushions, the phone off the hook, candles and nice aromatic oils (or incense) are good, but it's really up to you.
- Start by massaging, stroking and caressing your whole body then begin to stimulate any areas that give you a pleasant sexy feeling. These are your pleasure zones and could be your neck, ears and nipples, but they are different for different people so explore your own.
- You may then want to use a vibrator to stimulate your pleasure zones. If you haven't started already, you may want to stimulate your clitoris.
- Tease yourself with the vibrator. Stimulate yourself until you feel rushes of energy and tension throughout your body then back off and begin to stimulate yourself again until you orgasm. When you orgasm, restart pleasuring yourself within a minute.
- Move slowly to penetration and use the vibrator or your fingers to explore yourself. Stimulate the G Spot (found internally one-third to two-thirds of a finger from the opening of the vagina, on the front of the body just behind the pubic bone).
- Contract your PC muscles around the vibrator, or fingers, using whichever techniques and positions you have found to feel good.
- Continue to stimulate your clitoris throughout penetration, and ride your pleasure to another orgasm.
- Repeat as often, and for as long as you want!

## *Male multiple orgasm practice*

Here follows an exercise to help you achieve multiple orgasms. Practice as often as you can, as this will give you plenty of energy.

- Start by lubricating your penis with oil, or Vaseline. These lubricants do not dry up as quickly as saliva or body lotion.
- Begin to pleasure yourself however you like. Feel free to use erotic films or magazines initially, but try to use these to fuel your own fantasies. Your imagination is the uncensored testing ground for any fantasies you want to try out and can be far sexier than any film or photo ever produced!
- Pay close attention to the sensations in your body and your arousal rate. Be aware of the arousal as it intensifies: the tingling at the root of the penis,

the stages of erection, and how your breathing and heart rate increase as you build your orgasm.

- As you get closer and closer to the point of no return. Stop. Breathe deeply using your belly, and lightly contract your PC muscle around your prostate.
- Continue to pleasure yourself, coming increasingly close to the point of no return. As you get near to this point, go slowly. Start and stop arousing yourself more and more intensely, allowing yourself to fall back into an orgasm *without* ejaculation. Notice the involuntary contraction of your prostate (and anus) that occurs during this 'dry' orgasm. They may seem inferior in intensity to wet orgasms at first, but eventually with repeated practice they become powerful 'whole body' orgasms.
- After you have peaked several times without ejaculating, stop. Notice the feelings in your body and your energy levels. You should feel calm and energised with a tingling in your torso or head. This indicates you are on the way to whole body orgasms. Congratulations!

Note: At any point if you feel dizzy, or have any uncomfortable feelings then perform the *Inner Smile Exercise* (above). This will store any excess energy in your belly centre for use at a later date.

## Moving the energy up to the head

- Perform the 'inner smile' exercise outlined above.
- Move your hands down to cover your pelvis. Smile and bring the energy down to your sexual organs. Imagine the sun above your head, and begin to smile letting the corners of your eyes crease upwards. Feel your sexual organs growing warmer. If appropriate touch your genitals to increase the sexual energy, if this is not appropriate then simply think sexual thoughts.
- Once you start to feel the tingling and stirring of your sexual energy, begin to very gently contract your PC muscle, perineum and anus. This moves the energy into the lower spine.
- Imagine the energy rise up your spine, tucking your chin in to help it move from your spine to your head.
- Spiral the energy in your head using your imagination to create a vortex, and circle your eyes.

· Perform the Inner Smile exercise if you want to then store the energy in the navel.

## The spinal roll

If you feel the energy is not moving up your spine, try the following exercise standing, sitting or during orgasmic play. Stay aware of the energy levels in your torso and head, do not allow either to become overloaded with energy. If they do then use the *'Storing Energy In The Navel'* exercise above to shift it to your belly centre.

· Squeeze your anus up towards your tailbone, and rock your pelvis back and forth as if riding a horse.
· Draw your chin in and up and then back out in a soft gentle circle, keeping the jaw and neck muscles relaxed.
· After performing these exercises, rest and begin drawing the energy up your spine and into your brain. Look up with your eyes to help this process.
· Repeat until you feel the energy moves upwards, and then relax.

## Grounding

If you find you are not absorbing all the energy in your body, you feel restless or have expanded negative emotions try the following exercise.

· Sit in a chair, or lie on your back with the soles of your feet flat on the ground.
· Place your hands in front of your mouth so that your fingertips touch and your palms face your feet.
· Close your eyes and take a deep breath. Feel your stomach and chest expand slightly.
· Smile and exhale quietly, make the sound 'heeeeee'. As you exhale push your hands towards your feet. Imagine your body as a hollow tube filled with light that you are emptying with your hands from your head down past your torso, through your legs and out the soles of your feet.
· Repeat as necessary. If the problem persists seek advice from an acupuncturist.

Note: I cannot stress enough that all these exercises magnify the emotions already present within your body. Be aware of them, and if venting does not get rid of them there could be some sort of 'blockage' present. If this is the case then it could be physical or emotional and indicates you are in need of some healing. Seek a doctor, a therapist, an acupuncturist, a masseur, an osteopath, a herbalist, or any other healer you consider useful!

# Method – 'Powering and Feeding'

Select the glyph from your personal grimoire for the entity you wish to work with (See the Practicum exercises in 'Art' and 'Demons' above).

Prepare the space for the ritual with suitable music, lighting, incense, cushions and pillows etc. etc. for the particular entity you want to 'power up' through your glyph. Remember that the exercises magnify the emotions you are feeling, so magically it is important that you are feeling emotions appropriate to the entity.

1.  Once you are satisfied with your surroundings, obtain the glyph of the entity you wish to empower. Sit with the glyph in front of you for a few moments. Concentrate on it and notice the feelings that arise in you.
2.  Begin to perform the method of contacting the entity from the 'demons' section, above, until you clearly visualise the entity standing in front of you. Notice any changes in the space around you.
3.  Stand up, and perform the 'shaking' exercise for about 10 to 15 minutes.
4.  Perform the 'storing energy in the navel' exercise to clear your mind.
5.  Sit, lie or remain standing, but get comfortable. Make sure you can see the glyph (you may need to hold it in one hand, but this will restrict your movement).
6.  Begin to pleasure yourself as you did in the 'Multiple-Orgasm' practices.
7.  When you approach orgasm (without ejaculating for the men) draw the energy upwards using the 'moving energy up to the head' and 'Spinal Roll' exercises, as appropriate.
8.  Repeatedly approach (or have orgasms) until you feel you cannot hold back any more. Each time drawing the energy into your brain. Then one final time approach the orgasm and focus your attention on the glyph. Do not force energy into it; simply concentrate on its design totally as you orgasm. Do not hold back and let the energy created enter the glyph.

Note for the men: Do not get obsessed with the idea of ejaculating (or not) for the final time. It does not matter if you come or not. What is important is that you concentrate utterly on the glyph, moving towards it the energy created.

9.  Relax, and relish your orgasm.
10. Perform the 'Storing Energy In The Navel' exercise, and perform the 'Grounding' exercise if you feel you have excess energy.

This ritual can be used to power up all your glyphs. If you feel you need to perform it several times on a particular glyph then do so. Do not rush the period of time it takes to power them up, but do not let it drag and become boring either. This is supposed to be enjoyable, sexy and exciting. How much you allow it to be is up to you!

# Wedding

Note: The 'merging exercise' is described as a heterosexual encounter, but that does not mean a little bit of imagination cannot transform it into a powerful homosexual/lesbian/bisexual/transsexual one.

*Merging Exercise*

1.  Stimulate each other with foreplay.
2.  When you are both ready to continue sit facing each other (normally the woman is sat in the lap of the man) and begin penetrative sex.
3.  When the two of you are highly aroused draw back slightly so that the tip of the penis is inside the entrance to the vagina.
4.  Each partner should then exhale and contract your PC muscle. Try not to push each other over the edge into orgasm.
5.  Pump the energy up from your sacrum to the top of your head by contracting the PC muscle and anus.
6.  Rest and smile, allowing the energy to continue rising to your head.
7.  Spiral the energy in your head by rolling your eyes.
8.  Continue to make love, stopping when necessary to circulate the energy.
9.  When you are ready, you can exchange energy by the woman sending cool yin energy from her vagina and absorb hot yang energy from his penis. The man should simultaneously send hot yang energy from his penis to his partner, and absorb his partner's cool yin energy from her vagina. The two bodies begin to merge.

10. Draw your partner's energy back to your spine and up to the crown of your head, contracting the PC muscle if necessary.
11. Let the energy descend down the front of your head to your tongue. Touch tongues together, which closes the circuit and allows the energy to be exchanged through your mouth as well as your genitals.
12. Bring the energy down to your heart and exchange the healing love energy directly through your chests.
13. Smile as you focus on your navel and bring the energy down to your abdomen.
14. Repeat the exercise as appropriate, until you finally picture the image of you and your partner in sexual union above your head.

## Method - 'Merging The Path'

This method presented me with a real dilemma. When Rach and I performed the 'merging the path' we did it in a way, as both of us were essential to the rite. In our combined lovemaking both our criteria and desires were included in the final glyph created. The dilemma I am now presented with is - should I alter the rite to suit people who are without a partner? The more I try to alter it, the less it seems to fit. In the end I have decided to leave it as it stands because one of the themes I have enjoyed from doing this work is the realisation that I cannot do it in isolation forever and still remain content. We all want to be loved. If you are alone at the moment, concentrate on finding a trusted partner who will be more than happy to join you in this most beautiful of rituals.

Set aside at least 2 - 3 hours for this exercise. The more entities you have in your personal grimoire, the longer this will take. It really isn't worth doing this exercise until you have become familiar with the exercises on sex and can do the merging exercise above without thinking about it.
It is particularly demanding to do in one session, so don't worry if you want to spread the whole ritual over several sessions. If you fuck this up, and leave it half finished it could leave you feeling confused and unfocused. So ensure you finish it properly once the ritual has begun.

1. Assemble all the glyphs from your personal grimoire.
2. Adorn the temple in wonderful sexy, soft sensual fabrics and have sweet perfumed incense burning

3. Choose two different glyphs from either of your personal grimoires. Paint one of them on your partner's forehead, and allow them to do the same with the other on your forehead.

4. Sit facing each other and invoke into yourselves the entities these glyphs represent. Let them infuse and overwhelm your senses as far as you can.

5. Perform the 'merging exercise' together. As you allow the energy to circulate through your bodies concentrate on the glyph painted on your partner's forehead (your partner should do the same). Let this concentration deepen as you each approach orgasm, if you are male you must not come yet! Hold back your semen with PC clenches, let your body swim in post orgasmic delight.

6. Pause and stay relaxed. There is no rush. Combine the two glyphs that you painted on each other's foreheads in some way. Either by simply merging the two symbols, or include any visions, colours or sounds either of you had when merging. This should leave you with one glyph representing the two entities you have merged.

7. Allow your partner to paint this new glyph on your forehead.

8. Select a new glyph from your personal grimoire and paint this on your partner's forehead.

9. Repeat steps 4 – 8 until all the glyphs in your personal grimoires are 'merged'.

10. At the end of the ritual (or several sessions) you should have one glyph composed of all the entities glyphs in your personal grimoire. This is your glyph for The Path. The old glyphs are no longer useful as the entities they represent no longer exist.

11. Burn your personal grimoire with as much respect and ritual as you deem necessary.

# Death

1. Concentrate intently on the combined glyph for the path until you can see every detail of it without the physical glyph in front of you.

2. Lie back on the floor. Turn the phone off and ensure you will not be disturbed for a couple of hours.

3. Relax your body. Any muscles that are tense consciously allow them to relax. Close your eyes.

4.  Working your way up from your feet to the top of your head. Tense each muscle group in turn for about 2 seconds. Then relax the muscles. Feel them sinking slightly towards the floor.

5.  Now, concentrate on your breathing. As you breathe in let your awareness move to the back of your skull. As you exhale, feel your awareness move out with the breath to about 2 feet in front of your mouth. In towards the back of your skull and out with your breath. In and out.

6.  As you continue this breathing out allow the feeling in the extremities to disappear. Imagine a funeral pyre burning them to dust as they become numb. It's strange at first, but with repeated effort it becomes easier.

7.  Allow the funeral fire to burn your legs, arms, torso and head. Until there is nothing left of your body. Now concentrate on the glyph of The Path. Keep concentrating on it and nothing else as long as you can.

8.  When you become aware of your body again then keep the image of The Path central in your mind. Bring it through the veil from Death. Has it changed at all? Are there different colours or sounds associated with it?

9.  Incorporate any significant new sights, sounds or feelings associated with the glyph of the path and the Holy Guardian Angel.

10. Use this new glyph as a beacon to guide you in your life. It is the doorway to an entity that cares about you and wants to help you achieve your goals. Converse with it daily.

11. Burn the old glyphs for the path and the Holy Guardian Angel as they no longer truly exist. They have merged and become one entity.

12. Have a good life, and enjoy yourself because from now on you're on your own.

# Appendices

## Appendix 1

### Congruence

I want you to remember a time you really wanted something. Something you really looked forward to. I want you to see through your own eyes back in this experience, waiting expectantly for that special treat, present or event. Are there any sounds or feelings associated with this experience? If so then you remember them.

This is what it is like to be congruent. Play with the feelings, visual images and remembered sounds until you can re-enter the experience, and feel it as intensely as possible.

The feelings, sounds or visual images associated with this experience act as your 'congruence signal'. Remember this experience as you can use it to know when something is right. It is a good indicator of 'gut instinct', and can help in many choices.

# Appendix 2

Criteria

Criteria are the values that are important to us in a particular context. They are the reasons we do things, and what we get out of a goal once it is achieved. They are usually fairly vague like wealth, success, joy, health, love etc, but they determine where we work, where we live, the clothes we buy or where we spend our money.

Finding your criteria – Make a list of the ten most important values in your life. Sometimes it is useful to do this exercise with a friend or partner as they can question you, and if you are considering working together magically it is important to ensure you are both heading in the same direction. To do this simply change the word 'me' for 'us' in the following questions. The questions you should be asking are:

What is important to me?
What truly motivates me?
What has to be true for me?

Note: You should try to express the answers in the positive. I.e. instead of 'avoiding ill health' it would be better to phrase the value as 'maintaining good health'.

Once you have a list of criteria you need to find out what they mean in real, practical terms. You do this by finding out the evidence that lets you know the criterion has been met. This is not always easy to determine and may take some time, but the question to ask is:

How would you know if you got it?

Let's take 'health' for example. Will you have achieved good health when you can run a mile in 4 minutes, or will it be a feeling? Will good health mean you can do something you have not previously been able to do?

Finally you need to look at what this will mean to your present life.

How will your life change if you strive to achieve this criterion?

What will be the benefits?

Will you need to sacrifice something in order to achieve it?

What practical steps do you need to do to achieve this goal?

Repeat the above exercise for all the values you deem important.

Note: This is a classic Neuro Linguistic Programming (NLP) exercise, and for further reading on this subject see the 'Key Resources' section later in this book.

# Appendix 3.

Libidinal Energy

Libidinal energy is a term for energy arising from the libido.

*'Libido – A term originally used by Freud to refer to sexual energy which is derived from the id and is available to power mental and physical activity. Later Freud regarded libido as general life energy. In general usage, the connotation of sexual energy is still associated with the term'*
*- A Students Dictionary of Psychology, Arnold 1993*

The id is part of the unconscious personality, its function is to fulfil the instinctual needs but it operates according to the pleasure principle and may be satisfied by fantasising the desired object. I would suggest the Id can be guided to fantasise about particular goals through gnosis. The libidinal energy it produces can then be channelled into manifesting the goal in consensus reality.

I equate libidinal energy to the 'Chi' of Taoist philosophy and can be transmitted and channelled throughout the body (and beyond) by various exercises that combine the will with imagination.

*'According to the Tao, a brief burst of explosive energy occurs when a man or woman reaches orgasm. Western science has already established that, at the point of sexual orgasm, human brain wave patterns alter radically, literally putting the person into an 'altered state of consciousness.' Profound physiological and electrical changes occur through the system during orgasm, and a burst of energy is indeed emitted.' – Daniel Reid.*

However, having good sex is not the only way to generate this energy. It can be produced and generated by other means.

Eg, stand up, place your hands and fingers together, thumbs on top and fingers extended. Place them about four inches in front of your navel (As if you have clapped them together). Vigorously, rub your hands together forwards and backwards for two minutes.

The energy moving in your body can produce many physical effects. It could feel like a warm and tingly feeling, or you may describe it as a prickling, buzzing or humming sensation (like static electricity). Most people feel it moves slowly, especially at first, but it can sometimes move in a rush. It is important you do not try to force it.

To move the energy around you simply need to *focus your attention* on the place you want it to gather and increase. As the old Taoist saying goes:

'The mind moves and the Chi follows'

E.g., try the hand warming exercise again. After a couple of minutes of vigorous rubbing, stop, and sit down, relax and move your attention to your chest. Focus on your chest area, and notice the Chi moving to that area.

Important: You are not pulling or pushing the chi around. You are simply shifting your focus to another place. If you force the energy you can hurt yourself, so stay relaxed and soft. Besides the energy is easier to move if you're relaxed.

The applications and scope magically for this energy once created are limitless. Your attention is not limited to the confines of your body. And therefore the energy can be moved to objects and people, entities and beings that are perceived to be 'outside' your body. Think long on this and see if you can find magickal applications for it.

# Key resources

## Texts

*A Midsummer Nights Dream* – William Shakespeare

*Liber Null and Psychonaut* - Peter J. Carroll, Samuel Weiser, 1987.

*S.S.O.T.B.M.E. (Revised) An Essay On Magic* – Ramsey Dukes, The Mouse That Spins, 2000.

*American Gods* – Neil Gaiman, Headline, 2001

*Introducing Neuro-Linguistic Programming* – Joseph O'Connor and John Seymour, Thorsons, 1995.

*Pharmakon* – Julian Vayne, Liminalspace Publications, 2001.

*The Multi-Orgasmic Couple* (Sexual Secrets Every Couple Should Know) – Mantak Chia and Maneewan Chia, Douglas Abrams and Rachel Carlton Abrams, M.D., Thorsons, 2001.

*The Sandman: Dream Country* – Gaiman, Jones, Vess, Doran, Jones III and McKean, DC Comics 1990.

*The Hero With A Thousand Faces* – Joseph Campbell, Paladin, 1988.

*A Book Of Five Rings* – Miyamoto Musashi, Flamingo, 1974.

*Fear and Loathing In Las Vegas*, Hunter S. Thompson, Flamingo Modern Classics, 1993.

*World Tales*, collected by Idries Shah – The Octagon Press, 1991.

*Three Early Novels* – Philip K. Dick, Millenium, 2000.

*Visual Magick* – Jan Fries, Mandrake, 2000

*The Wonderful Story Of Henry Sugar* – Roald Dahl, Penguin, 1982.

*The Queen's Conjuror* – Benjamin Woolley, Flamingo, 2002.

Plus anything by the prophet Terry Pratchet. He disavows all links with 'magick', but whatever themes appear in our work as Chaos magicians subsequently appear in his books three months later. I let you draw you own conclusions!!

## Websites

www.liminalspace.co.uk

www.genesisp-orridge.com

## Sounds

*Leftism* by Leftfield

*Moonlight Sonata* by Beethoven.

*Preludes, Airs and Yodels* (A Penguin Café Primer)' by The Penguin Café Orchestra.

*Young Team* by Mogwai.

*The Moldy Peaches* by The Moldy Peaches.

*Levelling the Land* by The Levellers

*The Looks or The Lifestyle* by Pop Will Eat Itself

*Drumming* by Steve Reich.

*Ladies and Gentlemen We Are Floating In Space* by Spiritualized

# Notes

[1] At first the mind is taken up with learning the prose poem; when this is done so well that it is said automatically then the work can really begin.

[2] This is also the formula of witchcraft which is quite aptly given the 'dark and sinister' reputation of cults such as Quimbanda and Voudou. IAO=yod, aleph, ayin (10+1+70) = 81 which is 9 (the lunar number, Yesod) squared. 81 is also the number, by Hebrew Qabalah, of Witchcraft.

[3] Eshu are those spirits of the threshold – they are generally called on first during any ritual to act as messengers between the realm of humanity and of the gods (Orisha). Elegba or Legba is the personalised form of these entities as the god of the crossroads.

[4] Retrospectively a large part of this unnerving evening was due to poor preparation. I let myself loosen up by listening to some music by Mother Destruction. However I got rather pulled into a delightful Babalon evocation composition without really noticing what was going on. I hadn't banished the space properly and the Eshu spirits must have thought 'who is this dickhead?' (or something similar) and so decided to have some fun at the expense of my nerves!

[5] A Forelich Bose-Einstein condensate – see Zohar *The Quantum Self*, HarperCollins 1990.

[6] I found out that I was due to become a father not long after starting this working. Looking back I can tell that the conception coincided with the first day of the Ori working.

[7] A copy of the Ori $\Omega$ sign was added to the group fetish that was used during the Kali working (see later in this Volume).

[8] This technique formed part of a healing spell that had a miraculous effect.

[9] The master of one's head is an important concept in many of the African current systems. My Ori (through indirect means – ie networks of synchronicity) revealed mine to me during this working.

[10] Sections of this ritual were derived by Brother rhino from the work of various AMOOKOS adepts see for example Phil Hine see http://www.phhine.ndirect.co.uk/archives/tt_ganpuja.htm

[11] For the full text of this ritual see Razor Smile No1 see http://www.indifference.demon.co.uk/

[12] 3rd century Orphic Hymns – see *The Goddess Hekate*, Stephen Ronan (Ed), Chthonios Books 1992

[13] From Practising Transcendent Renunciation.

# Index

# Greg
# Humphries

## Julian Vayne

Printed in the United Kingdom
by Lightning Source UK Ltd.
101597UKS00001B/79-81